Ozarks
Travel
Guide 2025

Exploring the Heart of the Ozarks:
Scenic Drives, Outdoor
Adventures & Hidden Gems

Donald Clint

Table of Contents

Map of Ozarks

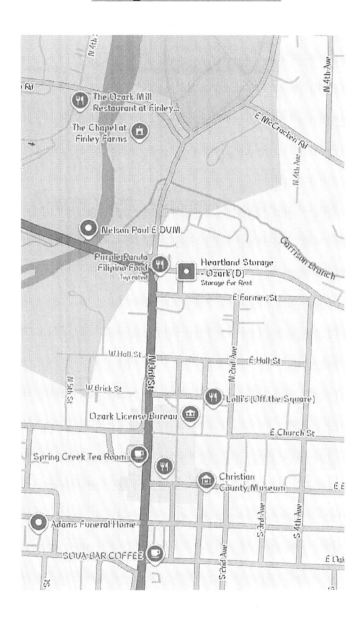

https://maps.app.goo.gl/SjqVJFawbBXu629W7

Scan the QR code to access the map on your mobile phone. You can do this using Google Lens or directly through your phone's camera app.

1. Welcome to the Ozarks

Introduction to the Region

Nestled in the heart of the central United States, the Ozarks is a vast and diverse region brimming with natural beauty, rich history, and vibrant culture. Spanning across southern Missouri, northern Arkansas, and reaching into small parts of Oklahoma and Kansas, this highland expanse is characterized by its rolling hills, deep valleys, pristine lakes, and an abundance of lush forests. Unlike the jagged peaks of the Rockies or the towering heights of the Appalachians, the Ozarks offer a unique landscape of rugged plateaus, intricate cave systems, and winding rivers that have carved their way through the limestone bedrock over millions of years. It is a region defined by its geological wonders, but also by the people who have called it home for generations.

The history of the Ozarks is as layered as the rock formations that shape its terrain. Long before European settlers arrived, Native American tribes, including the Osage, Quapaw, and Caddo, inhabited these lands. They thrived in the dense forests and along the rivers, relying on the region's abundant wildlife and natural resources for sustenance. Petroglyphs, burial mounds, and artifacts still found in the area today stand as silent testaments to their deep connection with the land. The arrival of French explorers in the 17th and 18th centuries marked the beginning of significant changes, as fur traders established routes through the region, and settlers from the East began to migrate into its valleys and hills. Over time, the Ozarks became a meeting ground of cultures—Native American, French, and Anglo-American influences all interwoven into the fabric of its heritage.

As the 19th century progressed, the Ozarks became a haven for pioneers seeking solitude, fertile land, and the promise of a self-sufficient life. Isolated homesteads sprang up across the hills and valleys, with families carving out an existence in harmony with the land. The Civil War left an indelible mark on the region, as battles and skirmishes were fought in its forests and along its rivers, shaping the communities that would emerge in its aftermath. The resilience of the Ozark people became a defining characteristic, as generations maintained their traditions, crafts, and ways of life even in the face of modernization.

Beyond its history, the natural splendor of the Ozarks remains one of its most captivating features. The landscape is dominated by the heavily forested Ozark Plateau, where oak, hickory, and pine trees stretch for miles, creating a haven for wildlife and outdoor enthusiasts alike. The region is home to some of the most breathtaking waterways in the country, including the crystal-clear springs of the Current and Jacks Fork Rivers, the meandering Buffalo National River, and the vast, man-made reservoirs such as Table Rock Lake and Lake of the Ozarks. These bodies of water serve as lifelines for local communities, providing opportunities for boating, fishing, and swimming, while also supporting an ecosystem teeming with fish, birds, and other wildlife.

One of the most striking geological features of the Ozarks is its extensive network of caves. The region boasts more than 7,000 known caverns, earning it the nickname "The Cave State" in Missouri. These underground marvels, such as the awe-inspiring Marvel Cave, the ethereal beauty of Blanchard Springs Caverns, and the depths of Fantastic Caverns, have long fascinated explorers and adventurers. Some of these caves have played a role in local legends, once serving as hideouts for outlaws, while others contain delicate formations that have taken thousands of years to develop.

While nature dominates the landscape, the cultural heartbeat of the Ozarks can be felt in its small towns, each with its own distinct character and charm. Branson, Missouri, often referred to as the "Live Entertainment Capital of the World," draws millions of visitors with its dazzling shows, family-friendly attractions, and deep-rooted musical traditions. The city's theaters host everything from country music performances to elaborate variety shows, showcasing a level of talent that has made it a beloved destination for travelers from all walks of life. Meanwhile, Eureka Springs, Arkansas, enchants visitors with its Victorian architecture, quirky art scene, and historic charm. Its winding streets and steep hills give the town a European feel, while its spiritual and healing traditions—rooted in its famous mineral springs—add a mystical allure.

The culinary landscape of the Ozarks is as rich as its history. Food in this region reflects a deep connection to the land, with farm-fresh ingredients and time-honored recipes playing a central role in local kitchens. Traditional dishes such as smoked barbecue, fried catfish, and biscuits with country gravy can be found in family-owned diners and roadside eateries. Ozark cuisine is also influenced by the foraging traditions of early settlers, with wild mushrooms, black walnuts, and fresh trout often making their way onto plates. A burgeoning craft beverage scene has also emerged, with local wineries, breweries, and distilleries offering unique flavors that reflect the region's agricultural heritage.

Music is another defining element of life in the Ozarks. The area has long been a stronghold for traditional folk and bluegrass music, with deep roots in old-time melodies brought over by early European settlers. Festivals celebrating the musical heritage of the region draw in crowds eager to hear the fast-picking banjo tunes, soulful fiddle harmonies, and heartfelt ballads that tell the stories of the people who call this land home. Whether in the small jam sessions on the front porches of country homes or in the grand stages of Branson, music remains an integral part of the Ozarks' identity.

As modernity continues to influence the world beyond, the Ozarks remains a place where history, nature, and tradition blend seamlessly. The region has managed to embrace progress while maintaining its distinctive character, preserving the untouched beauty of its landscapes and the warmth of its communities. Travelers who venture into its hills and valleys find a land that feels both timeless and welcoming, a place where the past lingers in the melodies of a fiddle tune, the craftsmanship of a handmade quilt, or the quiet majesty of a fog-covered river at dawn.

For those seeking adventure, tranquility, or a deeper understanding of America's heartland, the Ozarks offers an experience unlike any other. It is a land where every winding road leads to discovery, where the echoes of history whisper through the trees, and where the natural world stands as a testament to the enduring beauty of the American wilderness. Whether exploring its hidden caves, paddling through its pristine rivers, or simply soaking in the charm of its small towns, one thing remains certain—the Ozarks is a place that captures the spirit of exploration and the essence of home, all in one breathtaking landscape.

What's New in 2025

How to Use This Guide

The Ozarks continue to evolve, blending its rich traditions with exciting new developments that make each visit a fresh experience. The year 2025 brings a variety of additions and enhancements to the region, from new outdoor attractions and lodging options to expanded entertainment venues and culinary hotspots.

Whether visitors are first-time explorers or longtime enthusiasts of the area, they will find plenty of reasons to return and discover something new.

One of the most significant changes this year is the expansion of eco-tourism offerings. The growing emphasis on sustainable travel has led to the introduction of new eco-lodges and environmentally conscious guided tours that highlight the region's natural beauty while preserving its delicate ecosystems. More hiking trails have been added to both well-known state parks and lesser-explored areas, allowing visitors to experience the breathtaking landscapes from new vantage points. Several conservation efforts have also resulted in the restoration of native habitats, bringing back thriving populations of wildlife that had previously diminished. This resurgence of flora and fauna provides an even richer experience for nature lovers, who may now spot river otters, bald eagles, or even the elusive bobcat in their natural surroundings.

In addition to nature-focused expansions, 2025 has seen a surge in adventure-based attractions designed to offer thrill-seekers an exhilarating way to explore the region. New zipline courses stretching across deep valleys and over sparkling rivers provide breathtaking aerial views of the landscape, while updated rock climbing routes and bouldering areas cater to both novice and experienced climbers. Water sports have also seen an upgrade, with several new kayak and paddleboarding rental locations along the Buffalo National River and Lake of the Ozarks, making it easier than ever for visitors to immerse themselves in the water-based recreation that defines the area.

The entertainment scene has also evolved, with Branson unveiling several new shows and attractions that continue to solidify its reputation as a premier live entertainment hub. A newly constructed theater district brings cutting-edge technology to the stage, enhancing both classic performances and modern productions with immersive lighting, sound, and special effects. Long-standing favorite shows have introduced fresh acts and reimagined storylines, keeping audiences engaged while maintaining the nostalgic charm that draws visitors year after year. Meanwhile, Eureka Springs has expanded its arts scene, with an increased number of galleries, artisan workshops, and performance spaces that celebrate the creative spirit of the Ozarks. The town's well-known passion for eclectic and avant-garde art has led to the introduction of new festivals and exhibitions that showcase both local and international talent.

The culinary landscape has seen exciting developments as well, with a growing emphasis on farm-to-table dining and locally sourced ingredients. More restaurants now partner with regional farmers, bringing the freshest seasonal produce, meats, and dairy products to their menus. Food halls featuring multiple local vendors have begun popping up in key areas, offering an array of flavors that highlight both traditional Ozark cooking and contemporary twists on classic dishes. This expansion of dining options has allowed travelers to experience everything from rustic Southern comfort food to innovative gourmet creations, all while supporting small businesses and sustainable agriculture. Additionally, the craft beverage scene continues to flourish, with several new breweries and distilleries opening their doors and adding unique regional flavors to their offerings. Wineries have expanded their tasting rooms and vineyard experiences, drawing wine enthusiasts who seek to enjoy the picturesque landscapes along with finely crafted selections.

Accommodations have undergone notable transformations, with an increased focus on unique and immersive stays that allow visitors to connect with their surroundings in new ways. Luxurious glamping sites have been introduced, offering upscale tents, yurts, and even treehouses equipped with modern comforts, allowing travelers to be immersed in nature without sacrificing convenience. Traditional lodges and resorts have expanded their amenities, incorporating wellness experiences such as spa treatments that use locally sourced minerals and herbs, as well as meditation retreats that take full advantage of the region's tranquil settings. For those looking for something truly different, houseboats and floating cabins have become increasingly popular, providing a serene way to enjoy the waterways with the comforts of home.

In addition to these physical developments, digital advancements have also enhanced the travel experience. New mobile apps and interactive maps have been designed to help visitors navigate the region more easily, providing real-time information on everything from trail conditions and water levels to local events and dining recommendations. Augmented reality experiences have been incorporated into historical sites, allowing travelers to step back in time and witness reenactments of key moments in Ozark history through their smartphones or tablets. These technological innovations make exploring the area more accessible and engaging, especially for younger visitors and those eager to maximize their time with well-planned itineraries.

With so many new opportunities and enhancements available, understanding how to navigate the wealth of options can make a trip even more enjoyable. Approaching the Ozarks with a sense of adventure and curiosity will allow travelers to make the most of their visit, whether they are seeking outdoor thrills, cultural immersion, or peaceful relaxation.

One of the best ways to begin exploring is by considering the type of experience that best suits personal interests. Outdoor enthusiasts may wish to start with national parks, hiking trails, and waterways, while those drawn to history and culture can focus on historic towns, museums, and live performances. Culinary explorers will find satisfaction in researching farm-to-table dining spots and locally owned establishments that showcase the region's diverse flavors. Understanding the seasonal differences in the Ozarks can also enhance the experience, as spring and fall offer breathtaking foliage and mild temperatures, while summer is ideal for water activities, and winter brings a quieter, cozier retreat.

Being prepared for the natural environment is also key to a rewarding visit. Weather in the Ozarks can be unpredictable, with sudden changes in temperature and the possibility of rainstorms, particularly in the spring and summer months. Packing accordingly—layered clothing for changing temperatures, sturdy footwear for exploring, and insect repellent for wooded areas—ensures a comfortable and enjoyable experience. Visitors engaging in outdoor activities should always check local conditions before heading out, as river levels, hiking trail accessibility, and wildlife activity can impact plans.

For those traveling with family or groups, planning ahead can help accommodate a variety of interests. Many attractions offer guided tours, making it easy to gain deeper insights into the area's history, geology, and wildlife while keeping the experience engaging for all ages. Families with children may appreciate destinations that blend education with entertainment, such as interactive museums, wildlife parks, and outdoor adventure centers. Meanwhile, couples or solo travelers may find peace in the region's secluded cabins, scenic overlooks, and hidden hiking trails that offer a more personal connection to the land.

Transportation plays a crucial role in making the most of a visit, as the Ozarks' vast expanse means that having a reliable mode of travel is essential. While major cities like Springfield and Fayetteville have well-connected roads, venturing deeper into the hills may require navigating winding highways and backroads. Renting a vehicle suited for varied terrain can provide access to remote areas, while those preferring a more leisurely approach can take advantage of scenic byways that showcase the region's beauty at a relaxed pace. For those who enjoy the freedom of the open road, RV travel remains a popular way to explore, with numerous campgrounds and park facilities catering to mobile travelers.

Above all, embracing the spirit of exploration will lead to the most rewarding experiences. The Ozarks is a place where spontaneity often leads to the most memorable moments—whether stumbling upon a roadside farm stand selling fresh peaches, hearing an impromptu bluegrass jam session in a small-town square, or discovering a secluded waterfall along a forested trail. The balance of time-honored traditions and exciting new developments ensures that every visit offers something different, making each journey through the region one to remember.

2. Planning Your Trip

Best Times to Visit

How to Get There

The Ozarks is a destination that unfolds its beauty in different ways throughout the year, offering something unique in every season. Understanding the best times to visit depends on the kind of experience travelers seek, as the region's landscapes, activities, and weather conditions vary significantly across the calendar. While each season holds its own charm, some periods stand out as particularly favorable for outdoor exploration, cultural events, and comfortable travel conditions.

Spring emerges as one of the most captivating times to visit, as the landscape bursts to life with wildflowers, lush greenery, and flowing waterfalls fed by seasonal rains. From March through May, the temperatures are mild, ranging from cool mornings to pleasantly warm afternoons, making it an ideal time for hiking, camping, and wildlife spotting. Dogwoods and redbuds bloom across the hills, painting the scenery with delicate pinks and whites, while birdsong fills the forests as migratory species return. The rivers, revitalized by the melting winter frost and spring showers, flow with greater intensity, making this one of the best seasons for canoeing and kayaking. While occasional storms can bring heavy rains, they often pass quickly, leaving behind fresh, crisp air that enhances the outdoor experience. This time of year also sees fewer crowds compared to the peak summer season, allowing for a more peaceful connection with nature.

As spring fades into summer, the Ozarks takes on a different kind of vibrancy. June through August welcomes warm temperatures, long daylight hours, and an abundance of outdoor activities centered around the region's lakes and rivers. With highs often reaching the upper 80s and low 90s, water-based recreation becomes the highlight of the season. Boating, fishing, paddleboarding, and swimming draw visitors to places like Lake of the Ozarks, Table Rock Lake, and Bull Shoals Lake, where marinas and beach areas provide easy access to the water. The Buffalo National River, with its clear, cool waters winding through towering bluffs, offers the perfect setting for floating trips, whether by canoe, kayak, or tube.

Summer is also the peak of festival season, with live music, fireworks displays, and outdoor celebrations filling the calendar. Branson's entertainment district thrives during this time, offering a full schedule of shows and performances that appeal to all ages. While the warmth of the season is appealing, it also brings larger crowds, especially in popular tourist areas. Those seeking solitude may find better experiences in lesser-known hiking trails, secluded fishing spots, or early morning excursions before the midday heat sets in.

With the arrival of fall, the Ozarks transforms into a breathtaking spectacle of color. From mid-September through early November, the forests explode in shades of red, orange, and gold, creating some of the most picturesque scenery in the country. The cooler temperatures, often ranging between the 50s and 70s, make for perfect hiking conditions, and scenic drives along winding mountain roads become an unforgettable way to take in the beauty of the region. The Ozark Highlands Trail, Buffalo National River Trail, and the Glade Top Trail scenic byway are just a few of the places where travelers can witness the full glory of autumn.

Beyond the foliage, fall is a time when harvest festivals, craft fairs, and cultural events bring a sense of celebration to the area. Pumpkin patches, apple orchards, and corn mazes provide family-friendly fun, while local wineries and breweries often release seasonal specialties that capture the essence of autumn. Wildlife is also particularly active during this time, as deer, elk, and other animals prepare for the winter months, making it a prime season for photographers and nature enthusiasts.

Winter in the Ozarks is a quieter, more introspective season, yet it holds a distinct appeal for those who appreciate solitude and cozy retreats. From December through February, temperatures vary widely, with some years bringing mild, crisp air and others blanketing the higher elevations in light snowfall. While not known for extreme winter weather, the region does experience occasional frosty mornings and snow-dusted landscapes, particularly in the northern and higher-altitude areas. This season is perfect for visitors seeking peaceful getaways in remote cabins, where roaring fireplaces and scenic views offer a relaxing escape from daily life.

Branson embraces the holiday spirit in grand fashion, with elaborate Christmas light displays, themed performances, and festive events drawing in visitors from across the country. Eureka Springs, with its Victorian charm, also takes on a magical feel, as twinkling lights and holiday markets create an inviting winter wonderland. Outdoor enthusiasts who enjoy brisk air and quiet trails will find winter hiking a rewarding experience, as the bare trees reveal new perspectives on the land, and frozen waterfalls create stunning natural ice sculptures.

Getting to the Ozarks is an important consideration for travelers, as the region spans multiple states and encompasses both remote wilderness areas and bustling tourism hubs. While major cities like Springfield, Missouri, and Fayetteville, Arkansas, serve as common entry points, reaching more secluded areas often requires additional travel by car.

For those flying in, several airports provide convenient access to the region. The Springfield-Branson National Airport in Missouri is one of the primary gateways, offering domestic flights from major U.S. cities. Northwest Arkansas National Airport, near Fayetteville, is another key option, particularly for visitors exploring the southern reaches of the Ozarks. Smaller regional airports, such as Boone County Airport in Arkansas and Branson Airport in Missouri, also provide options for those looking to fly closer to their destination. Once on the ground, renting a vehicle is highly recommended, as public transportation within the Ozarks is limited, and many of the best sights are spread across winding, rural roads.

Driving remains the most popular and practical way to reach and explore the region. The scenic highways leading into the Ozarks offer breathtaking views and set the tone for the journey ahead. From the north, travelers coming from St. Louis or Kansas City can take major highways such as Interstate 44 or U.S. Route 65, both of which lead directly into the heart of the region. Those arriving from the south, such as Dallas or Little Rock, can follow U.S. Route 71 or Interstate 49, which provide direct access to the Arkansas portion of the Ozarks.

For road trippers seeking the most picturesque routes, the Ozark Mountain Parkway and the Pig Trail Scenic Byway offer stunning drives that wind through rolling hills, past dramatic bluffs, and alongside crystal-clear rivers. These routes not only provide beautiful scenery but also introduce travelers to charming small towns, historic landmarks, and hidden gems that might otherwise go unnoticed.

Once inside the region, navigating by car is essential for reaching more remote attractions, such as hiking trailheads, caves, and less-developed nature areas. While major roads are well-maintained, some of the most rewarding destinations require traveling along gravel roads or winding mountain passes. In these cases, having a vehicle suited for varied terrain can be beneficial, especially during rainy seasons when unpaved roads may become muddy or slick.

For those seeking a more leisurely approach to travel, some areas offer alternative transportation options. Branson features a trolley system that makes exploring its downtown and entertainment districts easy without the need for personal vehicles. Riverboat tours provide a unique way to experience the lakes and waterways, while guided excursions and shuttle services cater to visitors interested in specific activities such as cave exploration, winery tours, or off-road adventures.

Regardless of the method of arrival, planning ahead ensures a smooth and enjoyable journey. Checking seasonal weather conditions, understanding road layouts, and booking accommodations in advance—especially during peak travel periods—can help visitors make the most of their time in the Ozarks. Whether arriving by air or road, the journey itself becomes part of the adventure, setting the stage for the experiences that await in this captivating and ever-changing landscape.

Transportation Options

Budgeting & Costs

Navigating the Ozarks requires an understanding of the diverse transportation options available, as the region is vast, with a mix of well-developed highways, rural roads, and rugged trails leading to some of its most captivating destinations. While major cities and towns offer standard transit infrastructure, much of the area is best explored by personal vehicle, as public transportation is limited outside of urban centers. Those who plan their journey with flexibility and a willingness to embrace scenic drives will find that getting around is an integral part of the experience.

For travelers arriving from distant locations, air travel provides the most efficient way to reach the Ozarks before continuing by car. Several airports serve as primary gateways, each offering different advantages depending on the planned itinerary. The Springfield-Branson National Airport in Missouri is one of the most frequently used, providing connections from major U.S. hubs and a relatively short drive to key destinations. Northwest Arkansas National Airport, located near Fayetteville, is another common entry point, particularly for visitors exploring the Arkansas side of the region. Those seeking direct access to Branson can also fly into the Branson Airport, a smaller facility that caters to a mix of commercial and private flights. While these airports provide convenient access to the region, it is important to note that further travel by car is almost always necessary to reach specific destinations, as public transit options beyond city limits remain limited.

Once on the ground, renting a car is the most practical and commonly chosen method of transportation. The Ozarks' terrain is best navigated by private vehicle, as many of the region's highlights—secluded hiking trails, hidden waterfalls, remote cabins, and scenic overlooks—are located well beyond the reach of public transportation. Car rental agencies are available at major airports and within larger cities, offering a range of options suited to different travel styles. Those planning to explore off-the-beaten-path locations may benefit from renting a vehicle with higher clearance or all-wheel drive, as some gravel roads and mountain paths can become difficult to traverse after heavy rains. Gas stations are generally available throughout the region, but travelers venturing into more remote areas should ensure their tank is full before heading out, as refueling opportunities can become scarce in the deeper stretches of the mountains.

For those who prefer not to drive, limited alternative transportation options exist but require advance planning. In Branson, a trolley system operates within the downtown and entertainment district, offering a convenient way to move between attractions without the need for personal vehicles. Certain resorts and lodges also provide shuttle services to and from key points of interest, particularly for guided tours and excursion-based activities. Riverboat cruises and ferry services are available on some of the region's lakes and waterways, providing a scenic and leisurely way to experience the landscape from the water. While these options offer unique and enjoyable perspectives on the Ozarks, they are not a replacement for personal transportation, as they serve only specific routes and are not designed for general travel across the region.

For those seeking a more adventurous approach to transportation, biking and hiking provide an immersive way to explore certain areas at a slower, more intentional pace. The Ozarks is home to an extensive network of trails that cater to both cyclists and pedestrians, ranging from easy paved paths to challenging backcountry routes. Mountain biking has grown in popularity in recent years, with dedicated trails in areas such as Bentonville, Arkansas, and the Buffalo National River region offering world-class riding experiences. While biking can be a rewarding way to navigate shorter distances, it is not a viable option for covering large portions of the region, as roadways between key destinations are often winding, steep, and lacking dedicated cycling lanes.

Understanding the financial aspects of a trip is essential for making the most of the experience while staying within budget. Costs can vary widely depending on the style of travel, with options ranging from budget-friendly camping trips to luxury resort stays. While the Ozarks is generally considered an affordable destination compared to many other U.S. travel hotspots, prices fluctuate based on location, season, and the level of comfort sought.

Accommodations represent one of the most significant expenses, with a wide range of options available to suit different budgets. Budget-conscious travelers can find affordable lodging in the form of campgrounds, motels, and rustic cabins, many of which offer stunning natural surroundings at a fraction of the cost of high-end resorts. Camping fees at state parks and national forests are typically quite reasonable, with basic tent sites available for a minimal nightly rate. More developed campgrounds with amenities such as RV hookups, showers, and picnic areas tend to be slightly higher in cost but remain an economical choice. Motels and roadside inns provide another budget-friendly option, particularly in smaller towns where independent establishments often offer competitive rates.

For those seeking mid-range accommodations, a variety of family-run lodges, bed-and-breakfasts, and chain hotels provide comfortable stays without extravagant pricing. These options often include added conveniences such as complimentary breakfast, on-site dining, or access to nearby attractions, making them a good balance between affordability and comfort. Vacation rentals have also become increasingly popular in recent years, with cabins, cottages, and lakeside homes available for short-term stays. Renting a private home can be a cost-effective choice for families or groups, as shared expenses can lower the per-person cost while offering added space and amenities such as kitchens and outdoor fire pits.

Luxury travelers will find a growing number of high-end resorts and boutique accommodations that cater to those looking for a more refined experience. Upscale lodges offer premium amenities such as spa services, fine dining, and guided adventure excursions, while exclusive retreats in secluded settings provide privacy and personalized services. These accommodations come at a higher price but deliver an unparalleled level of comfort and exclusivity.

Beyond lodging, food costs can vary depending on dining preferences. Budget travelers can keep expenses low by opting for casual eateries, roadside diners, or preparing their own meals using local grocery stores or farmers' markets. Mid-range travelers will find plenty of reasonably priced restaurants featuring hearty Ozark cuisine, barbecue, and farm-to-table options. Those looking for a high-end culinary experience can explore fine dining establishments that showcase gourmet interpretations of regional flavors, often accompanied by extensive wine or craft beer selections.

Activity costs depend largely on the type of experiences sought. Many of the Ozarks' best attractions—hiking trails, scenic drives, waterfalls, and nature reserves—are free to access, making outdoor exploration an affordable option for budget-conscious travelers. State parks and national forest areas may require small entrance or parking fees, but these costs are typically minimal. More structured activities such as guided cave tours, boat rentals, ziplining, or live entertainment shows in Branson come with additional costs that can add up, particularly for families or larger groups. Planning ahead and prioritizing key experiences can help manage expenses without missing out on memorable moments.

Transportation costs should also be factored into the overall budget, with gas prices fluctuating seasonally and varying based on location. Those renting a vehicle should consider rental fees, insurance, and mileage costs, while travelers relying on shuttle services or guided tours should account for transportation fees when planning their expenses.

Overall, a trip can be tailored to fit a variety of budgets, from low-cost camping adventures to indulgent luxury getaways. Careful planning allows travelers to allocate funds toward the experiences that matter most while still enjoying the full breadth of what the region has to offer. Whether seeking an affordable escape into nature or a lavish retreat with all the comforts of modern hospitality, the diversity of options ensures that every visitor can create a journey that aligns with their personal financial preferences.

Top Destinations in the Ozarks

Branson, Missouri

Branson, Missouri, is a place where the scenic beauty of the Ozarks meets a vibrant entertainment scene, creating a destination that offers something for every kind of traveler. What was once a quiet town nestled in the rolling hills has transformed into a lively hub known for its theaters, attractions, and outdoor adventures. The city's unique blend of live performances, natural wonders, and family-friendly activities has earned it a reputation as one of the most dynamic vacation spots in the Midwest. Whether visitors come seeking world-class entertainment, outdoor recreation, or simply a relaxing escape in a picturesque setting, Branson provides an experience that is both exciting and deeply rooted in the charm of the region.

Entertainment is at the heart of Branson's appeal, and the city's famous theater district is a testament to its enduring status as a live performance capital. More than a hundred shows run throughout the year, covering a wide range of genres that cater to diverse audiences. Country music has long been a staple, with legendary performers and up-and-coming artists alike gracing the stages of iconic venues. Tribute shows honoring music legends such as Elvis Presley, Johnny Cash, and The Beatles bring nostalgic charm, while comedy acts, variety performances, and illusionists add to the ever-changing lineup. Many of these shows take place in venues along Highway 76, a stretch commonly referred to as the "Branson Strip," where bright lights and flashing marquees set the stage for an unforgettable night out.

Beyond its theaters, Branson is home to a variety of attractions that make it a favorite among families. Silver Dollar City, the city's premier theme park, combines thrilling rides with a celebration of 19th-century craftsmanship and Ozarks heritage. Set against a backdrop of wooded hills, this immersive park offers roller coasters, artisan demonstrations, and seasonal festivals that keep visitors coming back year after year. During the fall, the park's Harvest Festival showcases stunning pumpkin displays and live music, while winter transforms it into a glowing wonderland of holiday lights. Those seeking a more interactive experience can visit attractions like the Titanic Museum, where exhibits bring history to life, or WonderWorks, an upside-down science and amusement center that engages visitors of all ages with hands-on activities.

For those drawn to the natural beauty of the Ozarks, Branson provides access to an abundance of outdoor recreation. Table Rock Lake, a sprawling reservoir just minutes from the city, is a paradise for water lovers, offering opportunities for boating, fishing, swimming, and paddleboarding. Marinas provide rental services for those looking to explore the lake, while scenic trails along the shoreline invite hikers and cyclists to take in the breathtaking views. The Showboat Branson Belle, a paddlewheel riverboat, offers a unique way to experience the lake, combining dinner, live entertainment, and sightseeing into one memorable cruise. Nearby, Lake Taneycomo presents a cooler, spring-fed alternative that is especially known for its exceptional trout fishing, attracting anglers from across the country.

Hiking enthusiasts will find plenty of trails in and around Branson, ranging from leisurely nature walks to more challenging treks through rugged terrain. The Lakeside Forest Wilderness Area, located within city limits, provides a peaceful retreat with wooded paths, scenic overlooks, and waterfalls. Further out, the trails at Dogwood Canyon Nature Park lead through a pristine landscape of limestone bluffs, crystal-clear streams, and abundant wildlife. The park's guided tram tours offer an alternative way to explore its picturesque setting, giving visitors the chance to spot bison, elk, and longhorn cattle along the way.

Branson's dining scene reflects both its Southern roots and its growing reputation as a destination for diverse culinary experiences. Classic comfort food remains a staple, with barbecue joints, homestyle diners, and country kitchens serving up hearty portions of smoked meats, fried catfish, and biscuits with gravy. At the same time, the city has seen an emergence of more upscale and innovative dining establishments that cater to food enthusiasts looking for something beyond traditional fare. Farm-to-table restaurants highlight fresh, locally sourced ingredients, while steakhouses and fine dining venues offer elegant meals with views of the surrounding hills. For those looking to enjoy a drink with their meal, several wineries, breweries, and distilleries in and around Branson offer tastings and tours, showcasing the region's growing craft beverage scene.

Shopping is another popular pastime in Branson, with a mix of specialty stores, outlet malls, and artisan markets offering everything from handcrafted goods to name-brand bargains. The Grand Village Shops provide a charming collection of boutiques and locally owned stores, where visitors can find unique gifts, jewelry, and Ozarks-inspired home décor. Branson Landing, a waterfront shopping and entertainment district along Lake Taneycomo, combines national retailers with restaurants and live performances, creating a lively atmosphere both day and night. The Landing's fountains, which feature choreographed water and light shows set to music, add to the appeal, making it a favorite gathering place for both visitors and locals.

The city's rich history and cultural heritage are also on display in its many museums and historic sites. The Ralph Foster Museum, located on the campus of the College of the Ozarks, provides an in-depth look at the history of the region, featuring exhibits on pioneer life, Native American artifacts, and even the original truck used in the television series The Beverly Hillbillies. The Shepherd of the Hills Homestead, a historic site and entertainment complex, brings to life the setting of Harold Bell Wright's classic novel, offering visitors a glimpse into the area's past through live reenactments, horseback rides, and ziplining adventures.

Branson embraces the holiday season with enthusiasm, transforming into a winter wonderland filled with festive lights, themed shows, and special events. Christmas is one of the most magical times to visit, as the city's theaters debut holiday productions, Silver Dollar City lights up with millions of twinkling lights, and the Branson Scenic Railway offers a Polar Express-inspired train ride that delights children and adults alike. Parades, nativity scenes, and visits with Santa add to the charm, making Branson a top destination for holiday celebrations.

Accommodations in Branson range from cozy cabins tucked into the hills to luxury resorts with spa services and golf courses. Family-friendly hotels with pools and entertainment options cater to those traveling with children, while lakefront lodges provide a serene retreat for those looking to unwind. Many of the city's hotels and resorts are located near the entertainment district, offering easy access to theaters, restaurants, and shopping.

Branson's ability to blend entertainment, nature, history, and hospitality into one unforgettable experience is what keeps visitors returning year after year. Whether attending a world-class performance, exploring the great outdoors, or simply enjoying the warmth of a small-town atmosphere, the imagination and invites travelers to create lasting memories. Each visit to Branson offers new discoveries, whether it be a breathtaking sunset over Table Rock Lake, an unexpected connection with a local artisan, or the thrill of a live performance that transports the audience to another world. The city's ability to cater to a variety of interests ensures that no two experiences are ever the same, allowing both first-time visitors and returning guests to find something fresh and exciting with each trip.

One of the defining aspects of Branson is its deep sense of hospitality. The warmth and friendliness of the people who call this city home contribute to its enduring appeal. Whether engaging in conversation with a performer after a show, sharing a meal at a family-owned restaurant, or receiving travel tips from a local shopkeeper, visitors often leave with a sense of connection that goes beyond the attractions themselves. This welcoming spirit, rooted in the traditions of the Ozarks, enhances every aspect of a stay, making guests feel like more than just tourists—they become part of the Branson experience.

The city's commitment to preserving and celebrating its heritage is evident in the way it blends modern entertainment with time-honored traditions. The Ozark Mountain way of life is still very much alive in Branson, seen in everything from the craft demonstrations at Silver Dollar City to the storytelling traditions that inspire its theatrical productions. This balance between progress and preservation allows Branson to evolve while staying true to its roots, ensuring that the charm that first made it famous remains intact even as new developments enhance its appeal.

As Branson continues to grow, new attractions, restaurants, and experiences add to its already rich landscape, providing visitors with even more reasons to return. Development in the theater district introduces fresh productions alongside classic shows that have delighted audiences for decades. Expanding recreational opportunities around the lakes and trails make the city an even greater destination for nature lovers and adventure seekers. And with new lodging options catering to a wider range of travelers, from budget-conscious families to luxury-seeking couples, Branson continues to shape itself into a destination that remains relevant and inviting year after year.

For those who have never been, Branson is a place that surprises and delights. Many first-time visitors arrive expecting a simple entertainment town but leave having experienced something far more immersive—an energy, a landscape, and a culture that leave a lasting impression. For those who return, it is a place of nostalgia, where childhood memories resurface, favorite traditions continue, and new experiences are made with each visit. Whether exploring the city's natural wonders, reveling in the magic of live performance, or simply taking in the peaceful beauty of an Ozarks morning, Branson remains a destination where joy is found in every moment, and the promise of discovery is always around the next bend in the road.

Eureka Springs, Arkansas

Lake of the Ozarks

Eureka Springs, Arkansas, is a town unlike any other, a place where Victorian architecture, artistic energy, and the natural beauty of the Ozarks blend seamlessly to create an atmosphere of both charm and mystery. Tucked away in the hills of northwest Arkansas, this small yet vibrant community has long been a haven for travelers seeking relaxation, inspiration, and adventure. Its winding streets, lined with historic buildings and eclectic shops, set the stage for a destination that feels both timeless and ever-evolving. The entire downtown district is listed on the National Register of Historic Places, preserving the unique character that has drawn visitors for well over a century.

The town's origins are deeply tied to the belief in the healing properties of its many natural springs. In the late 19th century, people from across the country flocked to Eureka Springs in hopes of curing various ailments by bathing in and drinking from these mineral-rich waters. Though modern medicine has replaced such practices, the springs remain an integral part of the town's identity, with many of them still accessible via scenic walking trails and hidden grottoes. Basin Spring Park, located in the heart of downtown, serves as a gathering place where visitors can take in the serene surroundings and reflect on the town's history.

Art and creativity are woven into the fabric of Eureka Springs, making it a favorite destination for artists, musicians, and free spirits. Galleries showcasing local and regional talent are scattered throughout the town, featuring everything from fine paintings and sculptures to handmade jewelry and pottery. Street performers and live music add to the lively atmosphere, particularly during one of the many festivals held throughout the year. Events such as the Eureka Springs Blues Festival, the May Festival of the Arts, and the quirky Volkswagen Weekend bring together visitors and locals in a celebration of creativity and community.

Beyond the town's cultural appeal, the natural surroundings offer endless opportunities for outdoor exploration. The rugged landscape of the Ozarks provides a stunning backdrop for hiking, biking, and wildlife watching. The trails around Lake Leatherwood City Park are particularly popular, winding through dense forests and around a tranquil lake that is perfect for kayaking and fishing. For those seeking a more exhilarating experience, the cliffs and caves surrounding the town invite rock climbers and spelunkers to test their skills.

One of the most iconic attractions is Thorncrown Chapel, a breathtaking glass structure set within a wooded hillside just outside of town. Designed by renowned architect E. Fay Jones, this architectural masterpiece blends seamlessly with its natural surroundings, allowing sunlight to filter through the towering glass walls and illuminate the serene interior. Visitors often describe the experience of stepping inside as both spiritual and awe-inspiring, making it a must-see for anyone visiting the area.

The town's unique personality extends to its accommodations, which range from historic hotels and charming bed-and-breakfasts to treehouse cabins and underground suites. The Crescent Hotel, often referred to as "America's Most Haunted Hotel," is one of the most famous places to stay. Built in 1886, this grand Victorian structure boasts sweeping views of the Ozarks and a long history of ghostly encounters. Those who dare can join one of the hotel's popular ghost tours, which delve into its eerie past and the many legends that surround it.

Dining in Eureka Springs is an experience in itself, with a variety of restaurants that reflect the town's eclectic nature. Cozy cafés serve up fresh, locally sourced dishes, while gourmet establishments offer fine dining with a creative twist. Many eateries embrace the slow-food movement, emphasizing organic ingredients and sustainable practices. Whether enjoying a casual meal on a patio overlooking the hills or savoring a candlelit dinner in a historic dining room, the culinary scene in Eureka Springs is sure to impress.

Just as Eureka Springs embodies the artistic and spiritual essence of the Ozarks, the Lake of the Ozarks represents the region's spirit of adventure, leisure, and recreation. Located in central Missouri, this vast reservoir stretches over 90 miles and boasts more than 1,100 miles of shoreline, making it one of the most popular destinations in the Midwest for boating, fishing, and watersports. The lake's sheer size and diverse offerings ensure that visitors can find everything from lively entertainment hubs to quiet coves perfect for relaxation.

At the heart of the lake's appeal is its reputation as a boating paradise. Whether cruising on a pontoon, speeding across the water on a jet ski, or sailing into the sunset on a yacht, the lake provides endless opportunities for aquatic enjoyment. Marinas around the shoreline offer boat rentals, guided fishing charters, and everything needed for a day on the water. Fishing enthusiasts will find some of the best bass, catfish, and crappie fishing in the region, with tournaments held regularly throughout the year.

Beyond the water, the surrounding landscape is rich with opportunities for exploration. Ha Ha Tonka State Park, one of the most scenic spots in the area, features dramatic cliffs, sinkholes, caves, and the ruins of a turn-of-the-century stone castle. The park's trails lead to breathtaking overlooks, providing panoramic views of the lake and surrounding hills. Another popular attraction is Bridal Cave, a stunning underground cavern filled with stalactites, stalagmites, and crystal-clear pools. The cave's otherworldly beauty has made it a favorite for guided tours, as well as an unexpected yet romantic wedding venue.

The Lake of the Ozarks is also known for its vibrant dining and nightlife scene. Restaurants along the waterfront serve up everything from fresh seafood to classic Midwestern comfort food, often with the added bonus of outdoor seating that allows diners to enjoy spectacular views of the water. Many establishments offer live music, creating a festive atmosphere that extends well into the evening. Bars and lakeside resorts host events ranging from lively dance parties to laid-back acoustic performances, catering to both energetic partygoers and those seeking a more relaxed social scene.

For families, the area provides a wealth of attractions designed to entertain visitors of all ages. Water parks, mini-golf courses, and adventure parks ensure that kids have plenty to keep them engaged, while museums and historic sites offer educational experiences alongside the fun. Osage Beach, the main commercial hub of the lake, is home to a variety of shops, from boutique stores to sprawling outlet malls, making it a popular stop for those looking to indulge in some retail therapy.

Accommodations at the Lake of the Ozarks cater to every type of traveler, from rustic lakefront cabins and cozy cottages to upscale resorts with full-service spas and golf courses. Many vacationers opt for rental homes, which provide the convenience of private docks, full kitchens, and ample space for families and groups. Whether staying in a secluded retreat or a bustling resort community, the lake's diverse lodging options allow visitors to tailor their experience to their personal preferences.

The energy of the Lake of the Ozarks is palpable, with each season offering its own unique charm. Summer is the peak time for activity, when the lake buzzes with boaters and vacationers soaking up the sun. Fall brings a quieter beauty, as the hills surrounding the water burst into vibrant shades of red, orange, and gold. Winter, while less crowded, has its own appeal, with cozy lakeside cabins providing a peaceful retreat and holiday festivities adding warmth to the colder months. Spring marks the renewal of outdoor activities, as nature awakens and the excitement of the summer season begins to build.

Together, Eureka Springs and the Lake of the Ozarks represent two distinct yet equally captivating sides of the region. One is a sanctuary of creativity, history, and healing waters; the other, a playground of adventure, recreation, and lakeside leisure. Both destinations embody the timeless allure of the Ozarks, offering visitors unforgettable experiences shaped by the beauty of nature, the richness of culture, and the welcoming spirit of the people who call this region home.

Buffalo National River

Springfield & Beyond

Buffalo National River is one of the last remaining undammed rivers in the United States, a pristine waterway that meanders for 135 miles through the rugged Ozark Mountains in northern Arkansas. Protected as a national river, this natural wonder remains untouched by modern development, preserving its free-flowing course as it carves through deep limestone bluffs, lush forests, and expansive valleys. It is a destination that draws outdoor enthusiasts, nature lovers, and history seekers alike, offering a chance to immerse in the wild beauty of the Ozarks while exploring its abundant recreational opportunities.

Paddling along the river is one of the most rewarding ways to experience its breathtaking scenery. Whether by canoe, kayak, or raft, visitors can glide through gentle currents and thrilling rapids, passing towering cliffs and secluded gravel bars that invite peaceful moments of reflection. The river's three main sections—the Upper, Middle, and Lower Buffalo—each offer distinct experiences. The Upper Buffalo, known for its strikingly steep bluffs and faster-moving waters, provides a more adventurous route, particularly in the spring when water levels are at their highest. The Middle Buffalo features more moderate flows, making it a popular choice for beginners and families. The Lower Buffalo, where the river slows and widens, offers a tranquil paddling experience with abundant wildlife and opportunities for multi-day float trips.

Camping along the riverbank enhances the sense of adventure, with designated campsites and primitive spots available for those who wish to spend the night under a canopy of stars. The experience of sleeping beside the gently flowing water, surrounded by the sounds of nature, is one that many consider the highlight of their trip. Campers often wake to the sight of mist rising over the river and the calls of birds echoing through the trees, a reminder of the untouched wilderness that defines this area.

Hiking trails weave through the landscape surrounding the river, providing access to hidden waterfalls, caves, and scenic overlooks. The Lost Valley Trail is a favorite among visitors, leading to Eden Falls, a breathtaking cascade that tumbles into a moss-covered grotto. Further along the trail, a cave system invites exploration, with a small waterfall hidden within its depths. The Goat Trail, another popular hike, offers one of the most dramatic viewpoints in the region, leading to a narrow ledge along Big Bluff that rewards hikers with panoramic vistas of the Buffalo winding far below.

Wildlife thrives in the protected ecosystem of the Buffalo National River, making it a haven for those who appreciate the richness of nature. Elk, once nearly extinct in the region, were successfully reintroduced in the 1980s and now roam freely in the river's valleys, particularly around the town of Ponca, where sightings are common at dawn and dusk. Deer, black bears, wild turkeys, and bald eagles are also frequently spotted, adding to the sense of wilderness that permeates the area.

Beyond its natural wonders, the region holds a rich cultural and historical heritage. The remnants of 19th-century homesteads and mills can be found scattered along the river, offering glimpses into the lives of the early settlers who once made their homes in these remote hills. The ghost town of Rush, once a thriving zinc mining community, stands as a silent testament to a bygone era, with its abandoned buildings now slowly being reclaimed by nature. The Buffalo River is not just a place of outdoor adventure but also a living museum of the Ozarks' past, where the echoes of history blend seamlessly with the beauty of the present.

Just over an hour to the north, Springfield, Missouri, serves as a gateway to the Ozarks, blending urban convenience with access to the region's outdoor splendor. As the third-largest city in Missouri, it offers a mix of cultural attractions, historic sites, and modern entertainment while maintaining the warmth and hospitality characteristic of the area. Known for its vibrant arts scene, diverse culinary offerings, and proximity to natural wonders, Springfield provides an ideal starting point for exploration.

One of the city's most iconic attractions is the Wonders of Wildlife National Museum & Aquarium, a sprawling complex that showcases both the aquatic and terrestrial ecosystems of the world. Visitors can walk through immersive exhibits featuring marine life, North American forests, African savannas, and more, all designed to inspire a deeper appreciation for wildlife conservation. The adjacent Bass Pro Shops Outdoor World, the original flagship store of the outdoor retail giant, is more than just a shopping destination—it is a sprawling wonderland for outdoor enthusiasts, complete with massive aquariums, wildlife displays, and an indoor swamp.

History comes alive in Springfield through its many museums and heritage sites. The Route 66 Car Museum pays tribute to the city's connection to America's most famous highway, displaying a collection of classic and rare automobiles that tell the story of cross-country travel in its golden age. Wilson's Creek National Battlefield, located just outside the city, preserves the site of one of the first major battles of the Civil War west of the Mississippi. Walking the battlefield's scenic trails and exploring its visitor center offers insight into the conflict that shaped the region's history.

Springfield's dining scene reflects the diversity and creativity of its growing community. From traditional Ozarks comfort food to international flavors and farm-to-table eateries, the city's restaurants cater to every palate. Cashew chicken, a dish that originated in Springfield, remains a local favorite, blending Chinese flavors with a distinctly American twist. Breweries and coffee roasters add to the city's culinary appeal, with craft beer and locally roasted coffee playing an integral role in its food culture.

Outdoor enthusiasts will find Springfield to be a convenient base for adventure, with numerous parks, trails, and natural areas just minutes from the city center. The Springfield Conservation Nature Center offers miles of scenic walking paths through woodlands and prairies, while Fellows Lake provides opportunities for kayaking, fishing, and birdwatching. The Ozark Greenways trail system connects urban and rural landscapes, allowing cyclists and hikers to explore the rolling countryside at their own pace.

Beyond Springfield, the surrounding countryside is dotted with charming small towns and scenic drives that reveal the quieter side of the Ozarks. The town of Ozark, located just south of the city, is known for its antique shops, historic mills, and access to Finley River recreation. Further south, the James River and its winding tributaries offer secluded paddling experiences through a landscape of bluffs and hardwood forests. Those willing to venture further can discover the beauty of Mark Twain National Forest, a vast expanse of protected wilderness where hiking, camping, and wildlife observation are at their best.

The combination of urban vibrancy and natural beauty makes Springfield and its surrounding region a compelling destination for travelers seeking both culture and adventure. Whether exploring the depths of an immersive museum, savoring a meal at a locally owned café, or setting out into the hills and waterways of the Ozarks, visitors find that this area offers an experience that is as varied as it is memorable. From the untouched wilds of Buffalo National River to the modern amenities of Springfield, this stretch of the Ozarks offers a journey that moves seamlessly between past and present, solitude and excitement, discovery and relaxation.

4. Outdoor Adventure

Best Hiking

The Ozarks are a hiker's paradise, where rolling hills, towering bluffs, cascading waterfalls, and dense forests come together to create an unparalleled natural playground. This region is home to some of the most breathtaking trails in the Midwest, winding through remote wilderness areas, past crystal-clear streams, and up to panoramic vistas that stretch for miles. Each trail tells its own story, revealing the region's geological wonders, diverse plant and animal life, and the rich history of those who have traversed these paths for generations. Whether seeking a short scenic stroll, a challenging backcountry adventure, or an immersive multi-day trek, the Ozarks offer trails for every level of hiker, each leading to an unforgettable encounter with nature.

One of the most celebrated hiking destinations in the region is the Buffalo National River area, where miles of trails weave through some of the most dramatic landscapes in Arkansas. The Lost Valley Trail stands out as a favorite among visitors, leading hikers through a lush box canyon filled with towering limestone bluffs, dense foliage, and hidden caves. The highlight of this trail is Eden Falls, a stunning waterfall that tumbles into a moss-covered grotto. Just beyond the falls, an adventurous climb into a cave reveals a smaller, interior cascade, making this trek a rewarding exploration of the Ozarks' underground and surface beauty.

For those seeking an even greater challenge, the Goat Trail to Big Bluff offers one of the most breathtaking overlooks in the entire region. This narrow, rocky path follows a ledge along Big Bluff, which rises 550 feet above the Buffalo River. The view from the top is nothing short of spectacular, with the river winding through the valley below and layers of rugged mountains stretching to the horizon. Due to its sheer drop-offs, this trail is not recommended for those with a fear of heights, but for experienced hikers with steady footing, it provides one of the most awe-inspiring perspectives in the Ozarks.

The Ozark Highlands Trail is a bucket-list experience for serious hikers, stretching over 270 miles across northwest Arkansas. This long-distance trail traverses some of the most remote and pristine areas of the Ozarks, passing through deep hollows, over high ridges, and alongside sparkling streams. Hikers along this path experience the full breadth of the region's natural diversity, from towering oak and hickory forests to rocky glades and wildflower-filled meadows. The trail can be completed in sections or as a thru-hike, with multiple access points allowing for customized routes based on time and ability. Wildlife encounters are common, with white-tailed deer, wild turkeys, and even the occasional black bear making appearances along the way.

Missouri's portion of the Ozarks is equally rich in scenic hiking opportunities, with the Ozark Trail serving as its premier long-distance route. Stretching more than 400 miles, this trail system showcases the rugged beauty of the Missouri Ozarks, leading hikers through some of the most remote and unspoiled landscapes in the state. One of the most popular sections is the Taum Sauk Mountain segment, which takes hikers to the highest point in Missouri and past the spectacular Mina Sauk Falls, the state's tallest waterfall. The trail's rocky terrain and steep climbs make it a challenge, but the reward is a landscape of dramatic cliffs, shaded valleys, and stunning overlooks that capture the essence of the region.

Another must-hike trail in Missouri is the Devil's Backbone Wilderness Trail, located within the Mark Twain National Forest. This secluded and rugged trail offers a true backcountry experience, winding through dense woodlands and across ridges that provide sweeping views of the surrounding hills. Named for the jagged rock formations that rise along the route, the trail offers an opportunity to disconnect from the modern world and immerse completely in the raw beauty of the Ozarks.

Hikers looking for a less strenuous but equally scenic experience will find Ha Ha Tonka State Park to be a perfect choice. Located near the Lake of the Ozarks, this park features a network of trails that lead to natural bridges, sinkholes, and the ruins of a 20th-century stone castle perched high on a bluff. The Castle Trail provides an easy walk to the remnants of this once-grand mansion, while the Colosseum Trail takes hikers into a massive sinkhole surrounded by towering cliffs. The park's diversity of landscapes, combined with its fascinating history, makes it a favorite among both casual walkers and seasoned hikers.

Waterfalls are among the most captivating features of the Ozarks, and several trails lead directly to these hidden gems. The Glory Hole Falls Trail in the Ozark National Forest is one of the most unique, leading to a waterfall that pours through a perfectly round hole in the ceiling of a rock overhang. This natural wonder is best viewed after a good rain, when the water flows most dramatically, but the hike itself is a beautiful journey at any time of year.

Another stunning waterfall hike can be found at Hercules Glades Wilderness in southern Missouri. The trails here lead to Long Creek Falls, a cascading series of waterfalls set within a rugged, remote landscape. This area, part of the Mark Twain National Forest, is known for its solitude and unspoiled beauty, making it an ideal destination for those looking to experience the wilderness away from the crowds.

No matter the season, hiking in the Ozarks offers an ever-changing spectacle of natural beauty. Spring brings a burst of wildflowers and flowing waterfalls, summer fills the forests with deep green canopies, autumn sets the hills ablaze with vibrant reds and oranges, and winter reveals a stark, quiet elegance as bare trees expose dramatic rock formations and frozen cascades. The diversity of the landscape ensures that each trail, no matter how many times it is visited, offers something new with every journey.

Safety and preparation are key to making the most of any hike in the Ozarks. The terrain can be rugged, with steep climbs, rocky paths, and unpredictable weather conditions. Carrying plenty of water, wearing sturdy hiking boots, and being aware of trail conditions are essential steps for a successful hike. Many of the region's trails are in remote areas, where cell service is limited, so carrying a map and letting someone know your planned route is always a good idea.

The connection between the land and those who walk its trails is something deeply felt in the Ozarks. For generations, these paths have been traveled by explorers, settlers, and nature lovers drawn to the wild beauty and sense of freedom that these hills provide. Today, hiking remains one of the best ways to truly experience the essence of the region—to step into the depths of its forests, to stand atop its towering bluffs, to listen to the rushing of its clear waters, and to witness the untamed splendor of one of the most remarkable landscapes in America. Whether seeking adventure, solitude, or simply a deeper appreciation for nature, the trails of the Ozarks invite all who walk them to become part of their story.

Scenic Drives & Overlooks

Boating & Water Activities

The Ozarks are a region of breathtaking beauty, where winding roads lead through dense forests, past towering bluffs, and along the shores of pristine lakes and rivers. For those who prefer to take in the landscape at a leisurely pace, scenic drives offer an unparalleled way to experience the rugged charm of this unique part of the country. Whether traveling by car, motorcycle, or even bicycle, the network of scenic byways that crisscross the region provides countless opportunities to witness the

Ozarks' ever-changing scenery, from rolling farmland and historic small towns to dramatic overlooks that offer sweeping views of the hills and valleys below.

One of the most renowned routes in the Ozarks is the Scenic 7 Byway, which runs through the heart of Arkansas' mountain country, offering some of the most stunning views in the state. Beginning in the northern part of the state near Harrison and stretching southward, this drive winds through the Buffalo National River area, where limestone bluffs rise dramatically above the water. As the road continues, it passes through the Ozark National Forest and the Arkansas Grand Canyon, a vast, tree-covered valley that is particularly stunning in the fall when the foliage bursts into brilliant shades of red, orange, and gold. Along the route, roadside pull-offs provide perfect spots for capturing photos or simply pausing to take in the panoramic scenery.

In Missouri, the Ozark Mountain Parkway is another unforgettable drive, taking travelers through some of the most rugged terrain in the state. This route follows Highway 160, a road that twists and turns along ridges and through deep hollows, revealing breathtaking vistas at every turn. The journey offers glimpses of hidden waterfalls, crystal-clear springs, and vast expanses of unspoiled wilderness. For those who appreciate a more leisurely pace, stopping at one of the many small towns along the way provides an opportunity to experience the local culture, from antique shops to family-run diners serving classic Ozarks fare.

The Glade Top Trail in southwest Missouri is a lesser-known but equally spectacular drive. This gravel road, designated as a National Scenic Byway, runs for nearly 23 miles through the Mark Twain National Forest, offering stunning views of rolling glades, rugged ridges, and deep valleys. The trail is particularly beautiful in the spring when wildflowers bloom across the landscape and in the fall when the hillsides become a tapestry of autumn colors. With minimal traffic and a remote, untouched feel, this drive offers a sense of solitude that makes it one of the most rewarding scenic routes in the Ozarks.

For those seeking high-elevation viewpoints, the drive to Whitaker Point, also known as Hawksbill Crag, in Arkansas is a must. While the final stretch requires a short hike, the reward is one of the most iconic overlooks in the Ozarks. Perched on a rocky outcrop high above the surrounding valley, Whitaker Point offers a breathtaking panoramic view that has become one of the most photographed spots in the region. This area is particularly stunning at sunrise or sunset when the changing light casts a golden glow over the landscape.

Another unforgettable overlook can be found at Sam's Throne, a rock formation located deep in the Ozark National Forest. This site, a favorite among rock climbers, also provides one of the most dramatic vantage points in the area. From the top, visitors can take in sweeping views of the forested hills stretching endlessly into the distance, with rugged cliffs adding to the dramatic scenery. The road leading to Sam's Throne is an adventure in itself, winding through some of the most remote and pristine areas of the Ozarks.

While the scenic drives and overlooks offer stunning views of the Ozarks from above, the lakes and rivers of the region provide an entirely different perspective, drawing visitors to explore the landscape from the water. The Ozarks are home to some of the clearest and most beautiful waterways in the country, making them a haven for boating, fishing, kayaking, and other water-based activities.

The Lake of the Ozarks, with its sprawling shoreline and endless coves, is one of the premier destinations for boating enthusiasts. This massive reservoir stretches over 90 miles, offering a mix of lively waterfront areas and secluded inlets where boaters can escape the crowds. Whether cruising on a pontoon, speeding across the water in a powerboat, or paddling along the quieter edges in a kayak, there is no shortage of ways to enjoy this vast lake. The area is also home to numerous marinas, boat rental shops, and waterfront restaurants where visitors can dock and dine with a view of the water.

Further south, Table Rock Lake is another gem, known for its crystal-clear waters and picturesque surroundings. This lake is particularly popular among those seeking a more relaxed and scenic boating experience. With over 800 miles of shoreline, it offers endless opportunities for exploring quiet coves, fishing for bass and crappie, or simply anchoring in a secluded bay to enjoy the peaceful atmosphere. The nearby town of Branson provides easy access to boat rentals, guided fishing trips, and other water activities, making it a convenient hub for lake adventures.

For those who prefer the serenity of a river, the Current River and the Jacks Fork River, both part of the Ozark National Scenic Riverways, provide some of the best paddling experiences in the region. These rivers are famous for their pristine waters, flowing past towering bluffs, lush forests, and historic springs. Kayakers and canoeists can take in the scenery at a leisurely pace, stopping at gravel bars for picnics or exploring caves and springs along the way. The deep blue waters of the spring-fed rivers, combined with the striking limestone cliffs, create a landscape that feels almost untouched by time.

Another iconic waterway in the Ozarks is the Buffalo National River, America's first designated national river. This free-flowing river offers one of the most scenic and rewarding paddling experiences in the country, with sections suitable for both beginners and experienced kayakers. The upper stretches provide thrilling rapids, while the lower sections flow more gently, allowing for a relaxing float trip through some of the most stunning landscapes in the region. Along the way, paddlers can spot wildlife such as deer, bald eagles, and the famous elk herds that roam the river valley.

Scuba diving may not be the first activity that comes to mind when thinking of the Ozarks, but the region's deep, clear lakes provide excellent opportunities for underwater exploration. Table Rock Lake and Bull Shoals Lake, in particular, are known for their visibility, attracting divers to explore submerged forests, rock formations, and even sunken boats and structures. The relatively warm water temperatures make diving a year-round activity for those eager to see the Ozarks from a completely different perspective.

Fishing is another major draw, with the lakes and rivers of the Ozarks offering some of the best angling in the Midwest. Bass fishing is particularly popular, with largemouth, smallmouth, and spotted bass thriving in the region's waters. Trout fishing is also exceptional, particularly in the cold, spring-fed waters of the White River and the North Fork River. These rivers are known for their trophy-sized rainbow and brown trout, drawing anglers from across the country who come to test their skills in these legendary fishing spots.

Whether driving along a winding mountain road to a breathtaking overlook or setting out on the water to explore the hidden gems of the Ozarks' lakes and rivers, the region offers countless ways to experience its natural beauty. The combination of stunning scenic drives and world-class water activities ensures that visitors can take in the best of the Ozarks from every possible vantage point.

Camping & RV Parks

Wildlife Watching

The Ozarks offer an unparalleled experience for those who seek to connect with nature, and few activities bring visitors closer to the region's wild beauty than camping under the stars or settling into an RV park surrounded by breathtaking landscapes. With vast expanses of national forests, serene lakesides, and hidden hollows, the area provides a diverse range of camping experiences, from remote backcountry sites to full-service RV resorts with modern amenities. Whether travelers are looking for a rugged adventure deep in the wilderness or a comfortable retreat with easy access to outdoor recreation, the Ozarks deliver a variety of options to suit every preference.

Camping in the Ozarks immerses visitors in an environment rich with towering hardwoods, dramatic limestone bluffs, and the soothing sounds of flowing water. Many of the region's campgrounds are situated near rivers and lakes, providing a peaceful setting where campers can wake up to mist rising off the water and end the day with a campfire beneath a canopy of stars. The Mark Twain National Forest in Missouri and the Ozark National Forest in Arkansas are home to numerous campsites that allow for everything from primitive tent camping to sites with fire pits, picnic tables, and vault toilets. In more developed areas, campgrounds offer additional amenities such as electric hookups, showers, and even Wi-Fi, blending the convenience of modern comforts with the appeal of the great outdoors.

For those looking to camp near water, the Buffalo National River in Arkansas is a prime destination. Several campgrounds line the river, allowing visitors to set up tents or park their RVs just steps away from some of the most scenic paddling routes in the country. These sites provide easy access to the river's clear, free-flowing waters, making them ideal for those who want to combine camping with kayaking, canoeing, or fishing. Steel Creek Campground, with its towering bluffs and proximity to hiking trails, is particularly popular, offering a stunning backdrop for an unforgettable camping experience.

Table Rock Lake and the Lake of the Ozarks also feature a wide range of camping options, from secluded sites nestled in wooded areas to full-service campgrounds with boat ramps and marinas. At Table Rock Lake, the Army Corps of Engineers maintains several campgrounds that provide direct access to the water, making them a favorite choice for boaters and anglers. The Lake of the Ozarks, with its extensive shoreline, offers both public and private campgrounds, many of which cater to RV travelers with spacious sites, full hookups, and family-friendly amenities such as playgrounds, swimming areas, and nature trails.

For those seeking a truly off-the-grid experience, the Ozarks are filled with opportunities for dispersed camping, also known as boondocking. National forests and public lands allow campers to find their own secluded spot, where they can enjoy complete solitude amid the natural beauty of the region. These locations provide a sense of true wilderness adventure, allowing campers to wake up to the sound of birdsong, explore hidden waterfalls, and experience the profound quiet that comes from being far away from civilization. While dispersed camping requires careful planning and adherence to Leave No Trace principles, it is one of the most rewarding ways to experience the Ozarks in their purest form.

RV travelers will find no shortage of options in the region, with campgrounds catering specifically to those exploring the Ozarks by motorhome or travel trailer. Many of the RV parks offer full hookups, pull-through sites, and a range of amenities, including laundry facilities, on-site stores, and recreational areas. Branson, Missouri, is home to several highly rated RV resorts that provide a perfect balance of nature and entertainment, allowing visitors to enjoy the outdoors while being just minutes from the city's famous live shows, shopping, and attractions.

Beyond camping, the Ozarks are an ideal destination for wildlife enthusiasts who wish to observe the diverse array of animals that call the region home. The dense forests, rolling hills, and pristine waterways create a habitat that supports an incredible variety of wildlife, from majestic elk to elusive bobcats. Whether exploring remote trails, paddling along quiet rivers, or simply sitting quietly at a campsite, visitors have countless opportunities to witness nature in its most undisturbed state.

One of the most spectacular wildlife experiences in the Ozarks is observing the elk herd that roams the Buffalo National River valley. Once nearly extinct in the region, elk were reintroduced to the area in the 1980s and have since flourished, becoming one of the most iconic species in the Ozarks. Early mornings and late afternoons are the best times to spot these magnificent animals, especially in the fall during the rutting season when the haunting calls of bull elk echo through the hills. Popular viewing areas include Boxley Valley, where large groups of elk can often be seen grazing in the open fields, offering an unforgettable sight for nature lovers and photographers alike.

Birdwatchers will find the Ozarks to be a paradise, with hundreds of species inhabiting the forests, wetlands, and grasslands. Bald eagles are among the most sought-after sightings, particularly in winter when they migrate to the region's lakes and rivers to fish. The Lake of the Ozarks, Table Rock Lake, and Bull Shoals Lake are prime locations for spotting these majestic birds as they soar over the water or perch in tall trees along the shoreline. Spring and summer bring an abundance of songbirds, including warblers, tanagers, and woodpeckers, filling the forests with their calls and adding vibrant flashes of color to the green canopy.

White-tailed deer are a common sight throughout the Ozarks, often seen grazing in meadows or darting through the woods. These graceful animals are most active at dawn and dusk, making early morning or evening hikes the best time for sightings. In the more remote areas, patient observers may even catch a glimpse of a black bear, though these shy creatures generally avoid human contact. While bear encounters are rare, visitors camping in backcountry areas should take precautions by storing food properly and following guidelines for minimizing attractants.

The waterways of the Ozarks support an entirely different array of wildlife, from beavers constructing dams along creeks to river otters playfully gliding through the current. Snapping turtles, softshell turtles, and a variety of fish species thrive in the region's rivers and lakes, while wetlands and marshy areas provide habitat for frogs, salamanders, and waterfowl.

The diversity of the Ozarks' ecosystems makes it one of the best places in the Midwest for experiencing wildlife in its natural environment. Whether quietly paddling a secluded stretch of river, hiking through a dense forest, or sitting by a campfire listening to the distant call of an owl, visitors to the region are constantly surrounded by the wonders of the natural world. The opportunity to witness such an abundance of wildlife, combined with the chance to camp beneath a star-filled sky or settle into an RV site overlooking a peaceful lake, makes the Ozarks a destination that continues to draw those who seek both adventure and tranquility in the heart of nature.

5. Culture & History

Native American Heritage

Civil War Sites

The Ozarks are a region deeply shaped by history, with layers of cultural heritage stretching back thousands of years. Long before European settlers arrived, the land was home to indigenous peoples who left behind a lasting legacy that can still be seen today. The Native American presence in the Ozarks is evident in the artifacts, petroglyphs, and sacred sites that dot the landscape, as well as in the oral traditions passed down through generations. For those seeking to understand the earliest inhabitants of this rugged and beautiful region, exploring its indigenous history provides a profound connection to the land and its original stewards.

The Osage people were among the most prominent tribes to inhabit the Ozarks, establishing a strong presence in the region long before European contact. Known as skilled hunters and traders, they lived in villages along the rivers, following a seasonal cycle of hunting bison on the plains to the west and cultivating crops in the fertile valleys of the Ozarks. The Osage developed a deep spiritual connection to the land, which is reflected in the sacred sites that remain today. Many of these places hold cultural significance, serving as locations for ceremonies, storytelling, and rites of passage. Bluff shelters and caves throughout the region contain traces of their presence, with ancient rock art providing glimpses into their worldview and daily lives.

Several locations in the Ozarks offer opportunities to learn more about the indigenous history of the region. The Osage Historic Site in Missouri preserves the legacy of the Osage Nation, providing insights into their way of life before their forced removal to present-day Oklahoma in the 19th century. Exhibits and interpretive trails tell the story of how they thrived in the Ozarks, using the rivers for transportation and trade, while also showcasing artifacts that highlight their craftsmanship in pottery, beadwork, and weaponry. The site offers a moving perspective on the resilience of the Osage people, who continue to maintain their cultural identity despite the upheavals of history.

Another important site is the Rockhouse Cave in Petit Jean State Park, Arkansas, where visitors can see ancient petroglyphs created by the region's early inhabitants.

These carved images, depicting animals, humans, and abstract symbols, serve as a testament to the spiritual and artistic expressions of the indigenous people who once lived in the Ozarks. The significance of these rock carvings remains a subject of study, with many scholars believing they were used in religious ceremonies or as forms of communication among tribes.

Burial mounds and other archaeological sites across the Ozarks further highlight the presence of indigenous cultures that predate European settlement by thousands of years. The Cahokia culture, which thrived in the Mississippi Valley, extended into parts of the Ozarks, leaving behind remnants of their civilization in the form of earthen mounds and settlement remains. These sites provide evidence of complex societies that engaged in agriculture, long-distance trade, and the construction of monumental structures for ceremonial purposes. Today, efforts are being made to preserve and interpret these sites so that visitors can gain a deeper understanding of the indigenous peoples who once called the Ozarks home.

As European settlers moved into the Ozarks, conflicts arose between the native inhabitants and the newcomers. The forced removal of the Osage and other tribes in the 19th century, often through treaties that were signed under pressure, marked a painful chapter in the region's history. The infamous Trail of Tears, which saw the forced relocation of the Cherokee, Choctaw, and other tribes to Indian Territory, passed through parts of the Ozarks, leaving a tragic legacy that is commemorated at sites along the route. The Trail of Tears National Historic Trail, which follows the path taken by thousands of Native Americans during their forced journey westward, includes interpretive markers and preserved sites that honor their struggle and resilience.

In addition to its indigenous history, the Ozarks played a significant role during the Civil War, serving as a battleground for some of the most intense conflicts in the western theater of the war. The region's rugged terrain, dense forests, and strategic riverways made it a crucial area for both Union and Confederate forces, resulting in numerous skirmishes, raids, and full-scale battles. Today, the Ozarks are home to well-preserved Civil War battlefields, historic homes, and museums that offer a window into the turbulent years of the war and the lasting impact it had on the region.

One of the most significant Civil War sites in the Ozarks is Pea Ridge National Military Park in Arkansas. This battlefield, preserved as a national historic site, was the location of one of the largest engagements west of the Mississippi River. The Battle of Pea Ridge, fought in March 1862, was a pivotal conflict that helped secure Missouri for the Union and weakened the Confederate hold on the region. Visitors to the park can explore the battlefield through driving and walking tours, taking in key sites such as Elkhorn Tavern, which played a central role in the battle. Interpretive exhibits and reenactments provide a vivid account of the strategies employed by both sides and the sacrifices made by soldiers who fought there.

Another key Civil War site is Wilson's Creek National Battlefield in Missouri, where one of the war's first major battles took place in August 1861. Known as the "Bull Run of the West," the Battle of Wilson's Creek saw Union and Confederate forces clash in a struggle for control of southwestern Missouri. The battlefield today is meticulously preserved, with walking trails leading to important landmarks such as Bloody Hill, where intense fighting took place, and the Ray House, which served as a field hospital after the battle. The visitor center includes an extensive collection of artifacts, including weapons, uniforms, and personal belongings of soldiers, offering a poignant look at the human cost of war.

Beyond these major battlefields, the Ozarks were a hotbed of guerrilla warfare, with bands of Confederate and Union sympathizers engaging in hit-and-run attacks, ambushes, and raids on small towns. Bushwhackers and Jayhawkers, as they were known, often targeted civilians, creating an atmosphere of fear and uncertainty that lasted long after the war ended. The historic town of Newtonia, Missouri, saw two battles during the Civil War, and today, visitors can explore its preserved buildings and learn about the town's role in the conflict.

Several historic homes and museums throughout the Ozarks provide additional insight into the war's impact on the civilian population. The Old State House Museum in Little Rock, Arkansas, offers exhibits on the state's divided loyalties during the war, while the Ralph Foster

Museum in Branson, Missouri, contains artifacts related to the region's Civil War history.

The scars of the Civil War can still be felt in the Ozarks, as the conflict left lasting divisions among families and communities. Even today, many of the old homesteads, battlefields, and historic towns serve as reminders of the struggles that shaped the region. Exploring these sites provides a deeper appreciation for the history of the Ozarks, from the indigenous cultures that first inhabited the land to the settlers and soldiers who fought for their place in it. Whether tracing the paths of Native American ancestors, standing on a battlefield where history was made, or visiting a preserved home that witnessed the war firsthand, the Ozarks offer a powerful journey through time.

Historic Towns & Landmarks

Ozarks Folklore & Music

The Ozarks are a land where history lingers in every valley, town square, and weathered wooden structure. Throughout the hills and hollows, historic towns and landmarks tell the story of a region shaped by frontier resilience, economic booms and busts, and the enduring spirit of the people who have called this place home. From 19th-century mining towns and river ports to Victorian-era mountain resorts, these communities preserve the past while welcoming travelers eager to step back in time.

Eureka Springs, Arkansas, is one of the most well-preserved historic towns in the region, its winding streets and steep staircases leading visitors through a picturesque landscape of ornate Victorian buildings. The entire downtown is listed on the National Register of Historic Places, with structures dating back to the late 1800s when the town flourished as a health resort. Drawn by the belief in the healing powers of its many natural springs, visitors flocked to Eureka Springs in its early years, leading to the construction of grand hotels, bathhouses, and entertainment venues. Today, many of these buildings remain, housing boutiques, art galleries, and bed-and-breakfasts that maintain the town's old-world charm. The Crescent Hotel, famously known as "America's Most Haunted Hotel," continues to draw both history enthusiasts and ghost hunters eager to experience its legendary paranormal activity.

Down in Missouri, the town of Ste. Genevieve offers a glimpse into the colonial history of the Ozarks. Established in the early 18th century by French settlers, it is the oldest permanent European settlement in the state. The town's historic district is filled with rare examples of French colonial architecture, including vertical log homes with distinctive wraparound porches. Visitors can tour the Bolduc House and other well-preserved residences to see how early settlers lived, while the annual Jour de Fête festival brings Ste. Genevieve's history to life with period reenactments, traditional music, and artisan crafts.

Not far from Ste. Genevieve, the mining town of Bonne Terre stands as a testament to Missouri's lead mining industry, which helped fuel the region's economy for over a century. The Bonne Terre Mine, once one of the world's largest lead mines, now operates as an underground lake where visitors can take boat tours through vast caverns and explore submerged mining tunnels. The mine offers a fascinating look into the industry that shaped much of the Ozarks, and its unique underground setting has even made it a popular destination for scuba divers seeking an otherworldly experience.

Westward into the heart of the Missouri Ozarks, the town of Mansfield holds a special place in American literary history as the longtime home of Laura Ingalls Wilder. It was here that she wrote the beloved "Little House" series, drawing from her own experiences of pioneer life. The Laura Ingalls Wilder Historic Home & Museum preserves her house, personal artifacts, and handwritten manuscripts, allowing visitors to connect with one of the most iconic voices of rural America. The surrounding countryside, with its rolling fields and wooded ridges, remains much as it was in Wilder's time, offering a scenic and deeply nostalgic journey for those who visit.

Beyond the physical landmarks, the Ozarks are a region steeped in folklore and music, where stories of legendary outlaws, supernatural creatures, and larger-than-life characters have been passed down for generations. Oral storytelling has long been a tradition in the hills, with folktales blending fact and fiction in ways that reflect both the hardships and humor of Ozark life. Some of the most enduring legends revolve around Jesse James, the infamous outlaw who supposedly found refuge in the remote caves and hollows of the Ozarks. Though his death was officially recorded in 1882, some locals claim he faked his demise and lived out his days in secret among the hills, a theory fueled by supposed sightings and whispered family lore.

Another enduring legend is that of the Spook Light, a mysterious orb that appears along a rural road near the Missouri-Oklahoma border. Reports of the light date back more than a century, with countless witnesses describing a glowing ball that moves erratically across the landscape. Explanations for the phenomenon range from natural gas emissions to ghostly apparitions, but the mystery remains unsolved, drawing visitors eager to catch a glimpse of the eerie glow.

Beyond ghost stories and outlaw lore, the Ozarks are home to a musical tradition that is deeply rooted in the region's cultural identity. Ozark folk music evolved from the ballads and fiddle tunes brought over by early European settlers, blending elements of Scottish, Irish, and English traditions with American influences. The music, often played on fiddles, banjos, and dulcimers, became a vital form of storytelling, capturing the joys and sorrows of mountain life in haunting melodies and spirited dance tunes.

Branson, Missouri, stands as the modern heart of Ozark music, its theaters hosting performances that range from country and bluegrass to gospel and folk. While the city's entertainment scene has expanded to include a variety of musical styles, its roots remain firmly planted in the traditions of the Ozarks. The Ozark Mountain Music Festival, held annually in Eureka Springs, also celebrates this musical heritage, featuring performances by both traditional and contemporary folk musicians who keep the region's sound alive.

Square dancing and jigging, two dance forms closely associated with Ozark music, continue to be an important part of community gatherings and festivals. These lively dances, often accompanied by fast-paced fiddle tunes, provide a glimpse into the social customs of the region's past, when music and dance were at the center of rural life. In smaller communities, it's still possible to find local music jams where musicians gather to play old-time tunes, keeping the tradition alive in an informal and authentic setting.

The stories and music of the Ozarks are more than just remnants of the past; they are living traditions that continue to evolve and thrive. Whether through the historic towns that preserve the memory of early settlers, the folklore that weaves through every hollow and ridge, or the music that fills the air in theaters and dance halls, the Ozarks remain a place where history is not just remembered but felt. Visitors who take the time to explore these traditions will find themselves immersed in a world where the past and present blend seamlessly, creating an experience that is as rich and enduring as the hills themselves.

6. Food & Drink

Must-Try Local Dishes

Best BBQ & Southern Comfort Food

The cuisine of the Ozarks is a direct reflection of the region's rugged, self-sufficient past, where early settlers relied on what they could hunt, grow, and preserve to sustain themselves through harsh winters and unpredictable seasons. Over generations, these traditions have evolved into a distinctive food culture that combines elements of Southern comfort food, Midwest heartiness, and old-world influences brought by German,

French, and Scots-Irish immigrants. The result is a unique and deeply satisfying culinary experience where slow-cooked meats, hearty stews, freshly baked breads, and an abundance of locally foraged ingredients play a starring role.

Among the must-try dishes, few are as synonymous with the Ozarks as fried catfish. Freshwater rivers and lakes have long provided an abundant source of this mild, flaky fish, and the preferred preparation is to dredge it in cornmeal, season it generously, and deep-fry it to a perfect golden crisp. It is traditionally served with hush puppies—crispy, deep-fried cornmeal fritters—alongside coleslaw and tartar sauce. Some restaurants even offer all-you-can-eat catfish nights, where diners can indulge in as much of this local favorite as they can handle.

Another staple of the Ozark table is beans and cornbread, a dish born out of necessity but cherished for its simple, satisfying flavors. Pinto beans, slow-simmered with ham hocks or salt pork, develop a rich, smoky flavor that pairs perfectly with a slice of warm, buttery cornbread. In many households and diners, this dish is accompanied by a side of fried potatoes or greens cooked with bacon, making for a meal that is as nourishing as it is flavorful.

A lesser-known but equally important part of Ozark culinary history is the wild game that has sustained the region's inhabitants for centuries. Venison, squirrel, and wild turkey have long been part of traditional meals, often prepared in hearty stews or slow-roasted to bring out their rich, earthy flavors. One of the most iconic dishes is squirrel and dumplings, a rustic stew where tender squirrel meat is simmered with vegetables and topped with pillowy dumplings that soak up the broth. Though not as common on restaurant menus today, this dish remains a favorite among those who continue the hunting traditions of their ancestors.

For those with a taste for the sweet side of Ozark cuisine, no visit to the region would be complete without trying a slice of black walnut pie. Black walnuts, which grow in abundance throughout the Ozarks, have a bold, almost smoky flavor that sets them apart from their milder English walnut counterparts. When baked into a rich, gooey pie filling similar to pecan pie, they create a dessert that is both deeply satisfying and uniquely tied to the region. Many home bakers and small-town bakeries take pride in using locally foraged black walnuts, ensuring that each bite carries the distinct taste of the Ozarks.

Perhaps the most beloved category of food in the Ozarks, however, is barbecue. The region boasts a barbecue culture that blends the slow-smoked traditions of Kansas City with the tangy vinegar-based sauces of the South, resulting in a style that is uniquely its own. Pork is the undisputed king of Ozark barbecue, with smoked ribs, pulled pork, and pork steaks taking center stage. Many pitmasters use a dry rub before slow-cooking the meat over hickory wood, allowing the natural flavors to develop before finishing it with a sweet and tangy sauce.

One of the standout barbecue offerings is Ozark-style burnt ends, a specialty that originated with beef but has been adapted in the region to feature pork. These bite-sized pieces of meat, typically cut from the charred, caramelized edges of smoked pork butt or brisket, are basted in sauce and served with a side of baked beans or potato salad. Their crispy exterior and juicy interior make them a must-try for any barbecue lover.

Brisket, while more commonly associated with Texas-style barbecue, has also found a home in the Ozarks, with many barbecue joints slow-smoking it for hours until it reaches the perfect balance of smoky bark and tender, juicy meat. It is often served sliced or chopped, sometimes piled high on a sandwich bun with a drizzle of barbecue sauce and a side of pickles.

Ribs are another essential part of the Ozark barbecue experience. Whether you prefer them dry-rubbed or slathered in sauce, the slow-cooked, fall-off-the-bone tenderness of these ribs is a testament to the patience and skill of the region's pitmasters. Some establishments even offer "Ozark-style" ribs, which are cooked low and slow over native hickory wood, giving them a deep, smoky flavor that sets them apart from other regional styles.

Beyond barbecue, Southern comfort food plays a significant role in the Ozarks' culinary landscape. Chicken-fried steak is a staple at nearly every diner and family restaurant, featuring a tenderized beef cutlet coated in seasoned flour, fried to a crispy golden brown, and smothered in creamy white gravy. It is traditionally served with mashed potatoes and green beans, creating a meal that is as rich and satisfying as it is nostalgic.

Biscuits and gravy, another breakfast favorite, showcase the region's love for hearty, home-cooked meals. Fluffy, buttery biscuits are split open and smothered in a thick, peppery sausage gravy, often accompanied by eggs and a side of crispy hash browns. Many restaurants and cafés offer their own take on this classic dish, with variations that include spicy sausage, added cheese, or even a drizzle of honey for a touch of sweetness.

For those seeking a more unique regional specialty, Ozark pudding is a dish worth sampling. This old-fashioned dessert is a cross between a cake and a custard, made with apples, nuts (usually black walnuts or pecans), and a simple batter that bakes into a warm, spiced treat. Served with a dollop of whipped cream or a scoop of vanilla ice cream, it is a dessert that captures the rustic charm of Ozark cooking.

While traditional dishes remain at the heart of Ozark cuisine, modern chefs and home cooks have begun experimenting with fresh takes on classic recipes, incorporating farm-to-table ingredients and innovative techniques while staying true to the region's roots. Many restaurants now highlight locally sourced meats, organic produce, and artisanal cheeses, creating a dining experience that is both elevated and deeply connected to the land.

Food festivals throughout the Ozarks provide an opportunity to sample a variety of regional dishes while celebrating the culinary heritage of the area. Events such as the Rock'n Ribs BBQ Festival in Springfield, the Black Walnut Festival in Stockton, and the Bean Fest & Outhouse Races in Mountain View bring together local chefs, farmers, and food enthusiasts to showcase the flavors that define the region. Whether indulging in slow-smoked barbecue, savoring a homemade slice of pie, or experiencing the warmth of a home-cooked meal in a roadside diner, the food of the Ozarks offers a taste of history, tradition, and the enduring spirit of the people who have shaped this unique corner of America.

Wineries & Breweries

Farmers' Markets & Roadside Stands

The rolling hills, fertile valleys, and rich soil of the Ozarks have long made the region an ideal place for agriculture, and in recent decades, it has become increasingly well known for its wineries, breweries, farmers' markets, and roadside stands. From family-run vineyards producing small-batch wines to craft breweries experimenting with local flavors, the Ozarks offer a wide variety of drinks and fresh, locally grown foods that showcase the natural bounty of the land. Whether sipping a glass of wine overlooking the countryside or selecting produce straight from the hands of the farmers who grew it, visitors will find an abundance of flavors deeply rooted in the history and traditions of the region.

The Ozarks' wine industry has grown steadily over the past few decades, benefiting from the region's unique climate and soil composition, which allow for the cultivation of hardy grape varieties. Missouri, in particular, has a long history of winemaking that dates back to the early 19th century when German immigrants established vineyards along the Missouri River. Today, wineries in the Ozarks continue this tradition, with both classic and innovative wines being produced across the region. Many vineyards specialize in native grape varieties such as Norton, Missouri's official state grape, known for its deep, full-bodied red wines. Others grow hybrid varieties that thrive in the local climate, including Chambourcin, Catawba, and Vignoles, each offering distinct flavors that reflect the region's terroir.

The experience of visiting an Ozark winery is about more than just the wine—it's about the setting, the hospitality, and the opportunity to connect with winemakers who are passionate about their craft. Many wineries are located in picturesque countryside settings, with rolling vineyards stretching across the hills and tasting rooms that offer stunning views of the landscape. Some feature live music on weekends, wine and food pairing events, and even tours of their production facilities, allowing visitors to see the winemaking process from grape to bottle.

Several of the most notable wineries in the region have gained national recognition for their high-quality wines and welcoming atmospheres. Just outside Branson, one winery offers a rustic setting where guests can sample a variety of wines, from dry reds to sweet fruit wines, while overlooking the scenic Ozark hills. In the heart of Missouri wine country, another well-known winery produces award-winning Norton and Chambourcin wines, drawing visitors who come to enjoy tastings in a historic stone cellar. Further south in Arkansas, vineyards nestled in the foothills of the Ozarks offer unique selections such as muscadine and blackberry wines, capturing the flavors of the local landscape.

While winemaking has deep roots in the Ozarks, the craft beer movement has also taken hold in the region, with a growing number of breweries producing innovative and high-quality beers. These breweries draw on the region's agricultural heritage, often using locally sourced ingredients such as wild berries, honey, and even foraged herbs to create unique flavors. The brewing scene is diverse, with some breweries specializing in traditional lagers and ales, while others push the boundaries with experimental brews infused with everything from roasted pecans to Ozark spring water.

Visiting a brewery in the Ozarks is an experience in itself, with many offering inviting taprooms where visitors can sample a rotating selection of beers while enjoying the laid-back atmosphere. Some breweries are located in historic buildings, repurposing old mills or warehouses to create spaces that reflect the character of the region. Others take advantage of the natural beauty of the Ozarks, with outdoor beer gardens where guests can sip a cold brew while taking in views of the surrounding mountains and rivers.

For those who prefer something stronger, several distilleries in the Ozarks are carrying on the region's long-standing tradition of whiskey and moonshine production. Drawing inspiration from the bootlegging history of the area, these distilleries craft small-batch spirits using time-honored techniques and locally sourced grains. Visitors can tour the facilities, learn about the distillation process, and sample everything from smooth bourbons to fruit-infused moonshines that pay homage to the Ozarks' rugged past.

While the region's wineries, breweries, and distilleries offer a taste of the Ozarks in liquid form, the farmers' markets and roadside stands provide an equally rich experience for those looking to savor the fresh flavors of the land. These markets are at the heart of the local food movement, connecting small-scale farmers with the community and offering visitors the chance to purchase produce that is often harvested just hours before being sold.

Throughout the Ozarks, farmers' markets range from small gatherings of local vendors in town squares to bustling markets that feature dozens of stalls selling everything from fresh fruits and vegetables to homemade jams, artisan cheeses, and pasture-raised meats. Spring and summer bring an abundance of berries, tomatoes, sweet corn, and peppers, while fall markets are filled with apples, pumpkins, and pecans. Many vendors also sell baked goods, from flaky fruit pies to cinnamon-laced apple fritters, made using old family recipes that have been passed down for generations.

One of the greatest joys of visiting a farmers' market in the Ozarks is the opportunity to meet the people behind the food. Many of the farmers come from families that have been working the land for generations, and they are eager to share their knowledge and passion for sustainable agriculture. Some markets even offer cooking demonstrations and farm-to-table events where chefs showcase the best of what the season has to offer.

In addition to the farmers' markets, roadside stands are a common sight along the highways and backroads of the Ozarks. These small, often family-run stalls sell fresh produce, honey, and homemade goods directly from the source. Driving through the countryside, it is not uncommon to see stands offering juicy watermelons in the summer, crisp apples in the fall, and jars of local honey year-round. Some stands operate on an honor system, with a simple box for customers to leave their payment, reflecting the trust and hospitality that define the Ozark way of life.

For those looking to experience the freshest flavors of the region, u-pick farms offer a hands-on way to engage with the local food scene. Throughout the Ozarks, orchards and berry farms invite visitors to pick their own strawberries, blueberries, peaches, and apples, creating a fun and rewarding experience for families and food lovers alike. Many of these farms also offer homemade cider, jams, and baked goods, allowing visitors to take a taste of the Ozarks home with them.

Whether exploring a winery tucked into the hills, savoring a craft beer brewed with local ingredients, or selecting a basket of just-picked peaches from a roadside stand, the food and drink culture of the Ozarks is deeply connected to the land and the people who call it home. It is a place where tradition meets innovation, where flavors are shaped by the seasons, and where every sip and bite tells a story. Visitors who take the time to explore these offerings will not only enjoy some of the best food and drink the region has to offer but will also gain a deeper appreciation for the hardworking farmers, winemakers, and brewers who keep these traditions alive.

7. Family-Friendly Attractions

Theme Parks & Entertainment

Museums & Educational Experiences

The Ozarks have long been a destination for families, thrill-seekers, and culture lovers, offering a diverse blend of theme parks, live entertainment, and educational experiences. With attractions ranging from world-class roller coasters to immersive historical museums, the region provides visitors with endless opportunities for adventure and discovery. Whether spending the day at a theme park filled with exhilarating rides and live performances or stepping back in time at a museum that tells the story of the Ozarks' rich past, there is something for every traveler looking to be entertained and inspired.

One of the most beloved attractions in the Ozarks is the iconic theme park nestled in the hills, offering a perfect blend of high-energy excitement and old-fashioned charm. This park has been a staple of the region for decades, drawing millions of visitors each year with its thrilling roller coasters, family-friendly attractions, and live shows celebrating the heritage of the Ozarks. With an atmosphere that pays tribute to the region's pioneer past, the park transports guests to a bygone era, where craftsmen demonstrate traditional skills such as blacksmithing, glassblowing, and woodworking. Visitors can watch these artisans at work, gaining insight into the craftsmanship that once defined daily life in the Ozarks.

For those seeking heart-pounding excitement, the park's collection of roller coasters offers some of the most exhilarating rides in the country. From towering wooden coasters that race through the forested hills to steel rides that twist and loop at high speeds, there is no shortage of adrenaline-pumping attractions. In addition to its coasters, the park features water rides perfect for cooling off on hot summer days, as well as interactive play areas for younger children. Seasonal events add even more magic to the experience, with festive decorations, themed performances, and special food offerings that celebrate everything from harvest time to the holiday season.

Beyond the thrills of the rides, the park's live entertainment is a major draw for visitors. Musicians, comedians, and variety performers take the stage throughout the day, offering everything from bluegrass concerts to high-energy stunt shows. Many of the performances showcase the musical traditions of the Ozarks, with skilled instrumentalists and vocalists bringing the sounds of the region to life. During special events, the park hosts nationally recognized acts, adding even more excitement to its already impressive entertainment lineup.

While theme parks provide high-energy fun, the Ozarks are also home to a variety of other entertainment options, including world-class theaters that feature live music, comedy, and theatrical productions. These venues attract top talent from across the country, offering visitors the chance to see everything from country music concerts to Broadway-style productions. Many theaters focus on family-friendly entertainment, ensuring that audiences of all ages can enjoy a night of music, laughter, and storytelling. Some performances pay tribute to legendary artists, while others highlight the history and culture of the Ozarks, weaving together music and narrative to create a uniquely immersive experience.

For travelers looking to combine entertainment with education, the Ozarks offer a wealth of museums and cultural attractions that provide deeper insight into the region's past and present. From history and science to art and nature, the museums in the Ozarks cater to a wide range of interests, making them a perfect complement to the area's more action-packed attractions.

One of the most notable museums in the region is dedicated to preserving and sharing the story of the Ozarks, offering exhibits on everything from early Native American inhabitants to the pioneers who settled the rugged terrain. Visitors can explore artifacts, photographs, and interactive displays that bring history to life, gaining a greater appreciation for the challenges and triumphs of those who shaped the region. Many of the exhibits focus on the unique cultural traditions of the Ozarks, from folk music and storytelling to the art of handmade crafts.

Another must-visit museum in the region highlights the role of the Ozarks in American military history, showcasing exhibits on conflicts ranging from the Civil War to the present day. Through immersive dioramas, historical documents, and personal accounts, visitors can gain a deeper understanding of the sacrifices made by soldiers and the impact of war on the region. The museum also features an impressive collection of military vehicles, aircraft, and weaponry, offering a hands-on look at the technology used in past conflicts.

For those with an interest in science and nature, several museums and discovery centers in the Ozarks provide opportunities to learn about the region's geology, wildlife, and environmental conservation efforts. One such center focuses on the diverse ecosystems of the Ozarks, featuring live animal exhibits, interactive displays, and educational programs that teach visitors about the plants and animals that call the region home. Guests can walk through immersive exhibits that replicate the caves, forests, and waterways of the Ozarks, gaining a new appreciation for the natural beauty that surrounds them.

Art lovers will find plenty to admire in the Ozarks, with museums and galleries showcasing everything from traditional folk art to contemporary works by regional and national artists. Several museums in the area house impressive collections of paintings, sculptures, and mixed-media pieces, offering a glimpse into the creative spirit of the Ozarks. Many of these institutions also host rotating exhibitions, ensuring that there is always something new to discover.

For families traveling with children, hands-on museums and discovery centers provide engaging and interactive learning experiences. These attractions offer exhibits designed to spark curiosity and creativity, with opportunities for kids to experiment with science, explore engineering concepts, and even step into the shoes of historical figures. Many of these museums also offer special programming, including workshops, live demonstrations, and storytelling sessions that bring history and science to life in an entertaining way.

In addition to traditional museums, the Ozarks are home to a number of living history attractions that allow visitors to experience the past in a more immersive way. At these sites, costumed interpreters reenact daily life from different periods in history, demonstrating skills such as blacksmithing, farming, and candle-making. Visitors can step inside restored buildings, watch historical reenactments, and even participate in hands-on activities that provide a deeper connection to the past.

The variety of theme parks, entertainment venues, and museums in the Ozarks ensures that visitors of all ages and interests will find something to enjoy. Whether experiencing the excitement of a world-class roller coaster, enjoying a live music performance, or exploring a museum that sheds light on the history and culture of the region, travelers can expect to be both entertained and enriched by the experiences they encounter. These attractions not only provide fun and adventure but also help preserve the stories, traditions, and heritage that make the Ozarks such a unique and special place to visit.

Wildlife Parks & Zoos

Festivals & Seasonal Events

The Ozarks are a paradise for nature enthusiasts, offering a diverse range of wildlife parks and zoos that provide both education and adventure. These parks showcase the region's rich biodiversity, allowing visitors to experience up-close encounters with native and exotic animals in settings that prioritize conservation and environmental awareness. Whether exploring a sprawling wildlife refuge where native species roam freely, visiting a carefully curated zoo featuring animals from around the world, or walking through interactive exhibits designed to educate visitors about local ecosystems, these experiences offer a deeper connection to the natural world.

One of the most remarkable aspects of the Ozarks' wildlife parks is their emphasis on conservation. Many of these parks function as sanctuaries, providing safe havens for rescued or rehabilitated animals that can no longer survive in the wild. Guests have the unique opportunity to observe black bears, bald eagles, elk, and other native species in spacious enclosures that replicate their natural habitats. Some parks even offer guided tours that take visitors deep into the wilderness, where they can witness animals in settings that closely resemble their natural environment. These tours are often led by expert naturalists who provide insights into animal behavior, habitat preservation, and ongoing conservation efforts in the region.

Zoos in the Ozarks provide an equally enriching experience, showcasing a mix of local wildlife and exotic species from around the world. Some zoos focus on smaller-scale, interactive experiences, where guests can feed giraffes, pet kangaroos, or watch penguins waddle along rocky shores. Others house large, meticulously designed habitats that bring visitors face-to-face with tigers, elephants, and rare reptiles. Many of these zoos have robust educational programs designed to inspire curiosity and a sense of responsibility toward wildlife conservation. Visitors can participate in behind-the-scenes encounters, learning about animal care and rehabilitation efforts firsthand.

For families with children, the hands-on experiences offered by wildlife parks and zoos make for unforgettable memories. Petting zoos featuring farm animals, aviaries filled with colorful birds, and butterfly gardens that allow visitors to walk among fluttering wings create an atmosphere of wonder and discovery. Seasonal programming enhances these visits, with special events like nighttime zoo safaris, feeding demonstrations, and conservation workshops that make learning about the natural world an interactive adventure.

Beyond the structured experiences of wildlife parks and zoos, the Ozarks' vast network of forests, rivers, and protected areas provides ample opportunities for spotting wildlife in their natural habitats. National parks, nature reserves, and hiking trails wind through lush landscapes where deer graze, wild turkeys wander, and owls call through the trees. Some areas are home to rare and elusive species, including bobcats and river otters, offering patient and observant visitors the thrill of spotting these animals in the wild. Guided nature walks, birdwatching excursions, and eco-tours add an extra layer of education, ensuring that visitors leave with a greater appreciation for the Ozarks' delicate and diverse ecosystem.

Complementing the region's natural attractions, the Ozarks also host an impressive array of festivals and seasonal events that celebrate local culture, history, and traditions. These gatherings bring communities together and invite visitors to experience the spirit of the region through music, food, crafts, and outdoor activities. No matter the season, there is always a festival or event offering a glimpse into the heart of the Ozarks.

Spring is a time of renewal in the Ozarks, and festivals during this season reflect the region's vibrant natural beauty. Wildflower festivals draw nature lovers eager to witness meadows bursting with color, while arts and crafts fairs bring together skilled artisans showcasing handmade goods inspired by the landscape. Food festivals celebrate fresh, seasonal ingredients, with local chefs and farmers coming together to offer tastings, cooking demonstrations, and farm-to-table experiences. Many springtime events highlight the Ozarks' deep-rooted musical traditions, featuring live performances of bluegrass, folk, and country music that fill the air with timeless melodies.

Summer in the Ozarks is marked by lively outdoor celebrations, from music festivals that draw crowds for days of performances to rodeos that capture the region's cowboy spirit. The long, warm days provide the perfect setting for fairs featuring carnival rides, fireworks displays, and competitive events such as pie-eating contests and log-sawing challenges. Fourth of July celebrations in the Ozarks are particularly noteworthy, with parades, patriotic concerts, and spectacular fireworks lighting up the night sky over lakes and riverbanks.

As the leaves begin to change in autumn, the Ozarks take on a golden glow, making fall one of the most magical times to visit. Harvest festivals fill town squares with the scents of spiced cider and roasted nuts, while pumpkin patches and corn mazes invite families to embrace the season's festive spirit. Oktoberfest celebrations pay tribute to the region's German heritage with traditional music, hearty food, and locally brewed beer. Ghost tours and haunted attractions tap into the Ozarks' rich folklore, offering thrilling experiences that range from eerie storytelling sessions to interactive haunted trails.

Winter in the Ozarks transforms the landscape into a wonderland of twinkling lights and cozy festivities. Christmas markets brim with handmade ornaments, warm drinks, and holiday treats, while towns and theme parks put on dazzling light displays that draw visitors from far and wide. Caroling events, live nativity scenes, and holiday train rides create an atmosphere of warmth and nostalgia, capturing the magic of the season. Many areas embrace winter sports, offering ice skating, sledding, and scenic horse-drawn carriage rides through snow-dusted landscapes. New Year's Eve celebrations provide the perfect way to close out the year, with concerts, fireworks, and lively gatherings that bring together locals and visitors alike.

No matter when one visits, the festivals and seasonal events of the Ozarks offer an authentic glimpse into the region's culture and traditions. Each event is an opportunity to connect with local communities, sample regional cuisine, and enjoy the unique blend of history, music, and hospitality that defines the Ozarks.

Together, the wildlife parks, zoos, and seasonal celebrations of the Ozarks create a tapestry of experiences that blend adventure, education, and cultural immersion. Whether encountering majestic animals in a conservation park, exploring a zoo's interactive exhibits, or joining a town square filled with music and laughter during a festival, visitors to the Ozarks will find themselves drawn into the region's rhythm and charm. These experiences serve as a reminder of the beauty, heritage, and community spirit that make the Ozarks a destination like no other.

8. Arts & Shopping

Local Art & Craft Galleries

Best Souvenirs & Handmade Goods

The Ozarks have long been a haven for artists, craftspeople, and makers who draw inspiration from the region's breathtaking natural beauty, rich cultural heritage, and deep-rooted traditions. Scattered across the hills, valleys, and charming small towns are countless galleries, studios, and workshops where visitors can witness the artistic spirit of the Ozarks firsthand. These creative spaces offer a diverse selection of locally made art and handcrafted goods, from intricate wood carvings and hand-thrown pottery to woven textiles and delicate glasswork. Each piece tells a story of place, craftsmanship, and the enduring artistic legacy that thrives in this region.

Galleries in the Ozarks range from contemporary spaces showcasing modern interpretations of regional themes to rustic studios where traditional folk art continues to flourish. Many galleries are housed in historic buildings, repurposed barns, or log cabins, adding to their charm and authenticity. Walking into these spaces, visitors are met with an explosion of color, texture, and craftsmanship that speaks to the deep connection between art and nature. Paintings of rolling hills, misty rivers, and wildflowers capture the essence of the Ozarks' landscapes, while sculptures, metalwork, and ceramics reflect the rugged beauty and resilience of the land. Many artists use locally sourced materials, incorporating native woods, clay, and natural dyes to infuse their work with an authentic sense of place.

In addition to visual art, the Ozarks are known for their longstanding traditions of handcrafted goods that blend function and beauty. Pottery, one of the most celebrated crafts of the region, has been practiced for generations, with artisans using both modern and traditional techniques to create everything from decorative vases to durable stoneware. Many pottery studios invite visitors to watch the process unfold, from raw clay being shaped on the wheel to the final glazing and firing. Handmade quilts, another beloved art form, showcase intricate patterns and meticulous stitching, preserving a centuries-old tradition that continues to thrive in the Ozarks. These quilts, often crafted using techniques passed down through families, serve as both functional heirlooms and stunning works of art.

Woodworking is another hallmark of the Ozarks' craft scene, with skilled artisans creating finely crafted furniture, carved sculptures, and delicate wooden utensils. Many of these pieces highlight the natural grains and textures of local hardwoods such as walnut, oak, and cherry, emphasizing the beauty of the materials. Musical instrument makers also play a significant role in the region's craft heritage, producing hand-carved fiddles, dulcimers, and banjos that continue to fuel the Ozarks' storied musical traditions. Visitors can often watch luthiers at work, carefully shaping and assembling instruments that will go on to produce the unmistakable sounds of folk and bluegrass music.

Beyond galleries and workshops, local craft fairs and artisan markets offer another opportunity to discover the Ozarks' rich creative culture. These gatherings bring together artists and makers from across the region, creating a vibrant atmosphere where visitors can browse an incredible variety of handmade goods. Live demonstrations, from blacksmithing and weaving to soap-making and candle-pouring, provide an immersive experience, allowing guests to see the time-honored techniques that go into each creation. Seasonal craft festivals, held in towns and scenic locations throughout the year, add to the excitement, giving travelers the chance to take home one-of-a-kind souvenirs while supporting local artisans.

Finding the perfect souvenir in the Ozarks means seeking out items that reflect the region's natural beauty, cultural heritage, and artisanal craftsmanship. Handmade goods offer a far more meaningful alternative to mass-produced souvenirs, ensuring that each keepsake carries a story of the place and the hands that created it. Pottery, with its earthy tones and organic forms, makes for a lasting reminder of the Ozarks, whether in the form of a beautifully glazed mug, a decorative bowl, or a sculptural piece inspired by the landscape.

Locally woven textiles, including hand-dyed scarves, rugs, and tapestries, offer another distinctive keepsake. These pieces often incorporate natural fibers and traditional patterns, reflecting both the history and creativity of the artisans who make them. Hand-carved wooden items, from kitchen utensils and cutting boards to intricate figurines and walking sticks, highlight the skill of Ozarks woodworkers and make for treasured gifts.

For those drawn to jewelry, the Ozarks offer a range of handcrafted pieces featuring natural gemstones, silverwork, and intricate beadwork. Many jewelers incorporate elements such as turquoise, quartz, and river stones into their designs, creating wearable art that embodies the region's natural splendor. Leather goods, including hand-tooled belts, wallets, and bags, showcase the craftsmanship of local artisans and the durability of traditional techniques.

Food-based souvenirs are another way to bring a taste of the Ozarks home. Jars of locally sourced honey, homemade jams and preserves, and artisanal chocolates offer delicious reminders of the region's flavors.

Handmade soaps, infused with herbs, wildflowers, and essential oils, capture the scents of the Ozarks, while small-batch candles crafted with beeswax and soy provide a sensory link to the region's forests and meadows.

Many visitors also seek out hand-bound journals, illustrated maps, and locally authored books that capture the history, folklore, and natural wonders of the Ozarks. These items provide lasting memories of the landscapes, stories, and traditions that define the region. Whether purchasing a detailed print of a scenic overlook, a handcrafted musical instrument, or a bottle of locally distilled spirits, each item serves as a tangible connection to the place and its people.

The best way to explore the artistic and handmade offerings of the Ozarks is to visit studios and markets directly, where travelers can meet the makers, hear the stories behind their work, and gain a deeper appreciation for the skill and dedication that goes into each piece. Many artists are more than happy to share their inspirations and techniques, creating an enriching experience that extends beyond simply purchasing a souvenir. Whether wandering through a gallery filled with stunning landscapes, watching a potter shape clay into a functional masterpiece, or strolling through a craft market filled with the scent of fresh-cut wood and beeswax candles, the Ozarks' creative spirit is present in every handmade detail.

Bringing home a piece of the Ozarks is more than just a keepsake—it's a way to carry the region's artistry, traditions, and natural beauty into everyday life. Whether it's a quilt stitched with care, a carved wooden spoon that tells a story of craftsmanship, or a painting that captures the changing hues of the hills, these treasures serve as lasting reminders of a place where creativity thrives in harmony with the land.

Antique Shops & Unique Finds

Shopping Districts & Boutiques

The Ozarks have long been a destination for treasure hunters, antique enthusiasts, and those in search of unique, one-of-a-kind finds that tcll a story of the past. Scattered throughout the region, from the smallest rural towns to bustling city centers, are an array of antique shops, vintage markets, and specialty boutiques that offer an eclectic mix of items. Whether it's rare collectibles, handcrafted decor, heirloom furniture, or nostalgic memorabilia, the hunt for timeless treasures in the Ozarks is as much an experience as it is a shopping trip. The region's deep-rooted history, combined with the enduring craftsmanship of past generations, makes it a prime spot for discovering pieces that carry both character and authenticity.

Many of the antique stores found in the Ozarks are housed in historic buildings, repurposed barns, or family-owned shops that have been in operation for decades. Walking into these establishments often feels like stepping back in time, with shelves and displays filled with items that evoke a bygone era. Rustic furniture, from solid oak cabinets to hand-carved rocking chairs, showcases the artistry of 19th- and early 20th-century craftsmanship. Vintage kitchenware, including enamel cookware, Mason jars, and cast-iron skillets, appeals to those looking to bring a touch of nostalgia into their homes. Quilts stitched by hand, their intricate patterns and rich colors telling stories of the past, are among the most cherished finds in the region's antique markets.

Collectors of rare and historical items will find no shortage of treasures hidden among the shelves and display cases. Civil War artifacts, historic maps, and old photographs provide glimpses into the Ozarks' storied past, while vintage signs, advertising tins, and early editions of classic books offer a chance to own a piece of history. Many stores also feature locally made folk art, repurposed materials turned into decor, and salvaged architectural pieces such as old doors, window frames, and ironwork that make for striking statement pieces in modern homes.

Beyond antique shops, flea markets and vintage emporiums provide an even broader selection of goods, with multiple vendors selling everything from mid-century modern furniture to rustic farm tools and delicate china. These spaces are ideal for those who enjoy the thrill of the hunt, as treasures often lie buried beneath stacks of forgotten relics, waiting to be discovered. Some of the best finds in the Ozarks come from these sprawling markets, where a single visit might uncover everything from Depression-era glassware to hand-carved musical instruments.

For those with an appreciation for locally made goods, the boutique shopping districts of the Ozarks offer a wealth of artisanal products, curated collections, and unique designs that blend traditional craftsmanship with contemporary style. Many of the region's small towns have charming downtown areas lined with locally owned boutiques, each with its own distinct character and offerings. Handcrafted jewelry, made from sterling silver, turquoise, and river stones, reflects the natural beauty of the Ozarks, while custom leather goods, including bags, belts, and wallets, showcase the skill of local artisans.

Fashion-forward travelers will find that the Ozarks are home to an array of stylish boutiques carrying everything from bohemian-inspired clothing to rugged outdoor wear. Many of these shops feature designs created by regional makers, ensuring that visitors take home something both unique and locally inspired. Natural fiber scarves, wool sweaters, and hand-stitched denim pieces celebrate the traditions of slow fashion and sustainable craftsmanship. These pieces not only capture the essence of the Ozarks but also support local designers and small businesses dedicated to preserving traditional textile arts.

Home decor shops and specialty stores in the Ozarks provide endless inspiration for those looking to bring a piece of the region into their living spaces. From rustic farmhouse-style furniture to intricately woven baskets and hand-poured candles, these boutiques emphasize quality, authenticity, and artistry. Many shops carry work from regional potters, whose hand-thrown mugs, plates, and serving dishes add an artisanal touch to any kitchen. Handwoven rugs, stained glass accents, and repurposed wood furnishings highlight the creative ingenuity of Ozarks craftspeople who blend tradition with modern aesthetics.

In addition to home decor, the Ozarks' specialty shops cater to those looking for gourmet food products, natural beauty items, and handcrafted wellness goods. Small-batch soaps, infused with lavender, honey, and wildflowers, offer a sensory experience reminiscent of the region's natural landscape. Essential oils, beeswax candles, and herbal remedies crafted by local apothecaries provide a deeper connection to the land's botanical richness. Many of these products draw on generations-old recipes, blending traditional herbal wisdom with modern self-care practices.

For food lovers, shopping in the Ozarks is a chance to stock up on locally produced treats that capture the flavors of the region. Small gourmet stores and farm-to-table shops offer everything from homemade jams and jellies to smoked meats, cheeses, and freshly roasted coffee. Locally made chocolates, nut brittles, and honey harvested from Ozarks beehives make for perfect gifts and edible souvenirs. Many specialty shops also carry handcrafted kitchenware, including wooden spoons, ceramic bowls, and stoneware baking dishes, allowing visitors to bring a touch of Ozarks craftsmanship to their own culinary experiences.

Exploring the shopping districts of the Ozarks means not only discovering unique treasures but also experiencing the welcoming atmosphere of local businesses and shop owners who take pride in sharing their knowledge, stories, and recommendations. Unlike big-box retailers, these independent stores offer a personalized shopping experience, where guests can learn about the history behind a vintage find, the process behind a handmade piece, or the best ways to incorporate locally made products into their daily lives. Many shop owners are artists themselves, creating a direct connection between the maker and the buyer that adds even more meaning to each purchase.

Seasonal shopping events, including holiday markets, antique fairs, and craft festivals, add to the excitement of finding something special in the Ozarks. These events bring together a variety of vendors and artisans, creating a vibrant and festive atmosphere where visitors can browse unique offerings while enjoying live music, local food, and a true sense of community. Whether visiting in the fall when pumpkin spice candles and cozy wool blankets fill the shelves; or in the spring when fresh floral arrangements and pastel ceramics make their debut, there's always something new and exciting to discover.

The experience of shopping in the Ozarks is as much about the journey as it is about the treasures found along the way. From small-town antique shops filled with forgotten heirlooms to boutique storefronts showcasing the latest in local design, every stop offers a glimpse into the region's creativity, history, and culture. Whether searching for a statement piece for the home, a wearable work of art, or a handcrafted memento that embodies the spirit of the Ozarks, the region's shopping destinations provide endless opportunities for discovery. Bringing home a piece of the Ozarks isn't just about acquiring an item it's about carrying a piece of its story, its artistry, and its soul.

9. Where to Stay

Luxury Resorts & Lodges

Cozy Cabins & B&Bs

The Ozarks offer an exceptional range of accommodations that cater to every kind of traveler, from those seeking indulgence in luxury resorts and high-end lodges to those longing for the quiet charm of cozy cabins and intimate bed-and-breakfasts. Whether positioned along the tranquil shores of a lake, tucked away in the heart of dense woodlands, or perched atop scenic bluffs with panoramic views, the region's accommodations blend comfort with the breathtaking beauty of nature. Guests find themselves immersed in an atmosphere that seamlessly combines rustic charm with modern amenities, ensuring a stay that is both rejuvenating and memorable.

For travelers looking for an upscale retreat, the Ozarks boast a selection of luxury resorts that provide world-class service, exquisite accommodations, and a wealth of on-site amenities designed for relaxation and recreation. These resorts often occupy prime locations, with private access to lakes, rivers, and rolling hills, offering guests an immersive nature experience without sacrificing comfort. Expansive suites and private villas feature elegant furnishings, plush bedding, and floor-to-ceiling windows that frame the stunning surroundings. Many resorts offer private balconies, outdoor hot tubs, and spa-like bathrooms, allowing visitors to unwind in style.

Beyond lavish accommodations, luxury resorts in the Ozarks place an emphasis on personalized experiences and high-end services. Spa treatments, including deep-tissue massages, facials, and body wraps, are often available, with many wellness centers incorporating local ingredients such as mineral-rich clays, herbal infusions, and Ozarks spring water into their treatments. For those who enjoy an active lifestyle, fitness centers, yoga pavilions, and guided nature walks provide opportunities to stay energized while enjoying the natural landscape. Golf courses nestled within the hills offer championship-level play with sweeping views, while private boat docks and fishing excursions provide guests with exclusive access to the region's pristine waters.

Culinary excellence is another defining feature of the Ozarks' luxury accommodations, with fine dining restaurants showcasing farm-to-table cuisine that highlights regional ingredients. Expertly crafted menus include locally sourced meats, seasonal vegetables, and freshly caught fish, often paired with wines from nearby vineyards or craft cocktails infused with botanicals native to the Ozarks. Many resorts also offer private dining experiences, with lakeside candlelit dinners, chef's table tastings, or gourmet picnic baskets designed for scenic outings.

For those who prefer a more intimate lodging experience that still exudes charm and elegance, the Ozarks' collection of high-end lodges provides a perfect blend of rustic sophistication. These lodges, often built with native stone and reclaimed wood, embrace the region's natural beauty while offering modern comforts such as high-thread-count linens, spa-inspired bathrooms, and fireplaces that add warmth and ambiance. Guests can relax on wraparound porches, take in the sounds of wildlife, or enjoy a peaceful evening by an outdoor firepit beneath the stars.

Lodges in the Ozarks cater to a range of travelers, from couples looking for a romantic escape to families seeking adventure and relaxation. Many lodges offer outdoor activities such as guided hiking tours, horseback riding, and kayaking excursions, allowing guests to experience the landscape up close. Wildlife viewing is a popular attraction, with some lodges offering binoculars and guided wildlife walks for guests hoping to catch a glimpse of deer, bald eagles, or even black bears in their natural habitat.

For travelers who seek solitude and a deeper connection to nature, cozy cabins scattered throughout the Ozarks provide a retreat that feels like home away from home. These cabins range from rustic and simple to luxurious and well-appointed, with many featuring wood-burning fireplaces, fully equipped kitchens, and private hot tubs overlooking scenic vistas. The appeal of cabin stays lies in their ability to offer privacy and tranquility, making them an ideal choice for couples, families, and solo adventurers alike.

Lakeside cabins provide direct access to the water, making them a favorite for fishing enthusiasts, kayakers, and those who enjoy waking up to the gentle lapping of waves against the shore. Many cabins include private docks, allowing guests to launch boats or simply relax on the water's edge with a morning coffee in hand. For those drawn to the mountains, hillside cabins offer breathtaking views of rolling forests and mist-covered peaks, creating an unparalleled sense of seclusion and serenity.

One of the defining features of cabin stays in the Ozarks is the opportunity to experience the simple pleasures of life at a slower pace. Guests can curl up with a book by the fire, prepare meals with fresh ingredients from local markets, or gather around a fire pit for an evening of storytelling and stargazing. Unlike larger resorts, cabins allow for a more personalized and flexible experience, where travelers can set their own schedules and embrace the rhythm of nature.

For those who prefer a mix of comfort and social engagement, the Ozarks' bed-and-breakfasts provide a welcoming and homey atmosphere infused with local charm. Often housed in historic buildings, converted farmhouses, or Victorian-era mansions, these accommodations offer a glimpse into the region's history and hospitality. Guests are treated to homemade breakfasts featuring local specialties such as buttermilk biscuits, country ham, and seasonal fruit preserves, all served with warm conversation and insider tips from knowledgeable hosts.

Bed-and-breakfasts in the Ozarks vary in style and ambiance, from elegant inns with antique furnishings and manicured gardens to casual country retreats with rocking chairs on the porch and farm animals roaming nearby. Each offers a unique experience, whether it's a romantic weekend in a rose-covered cottage, a stay in a family-friendly farmhouse, or a getaway in a lakeside inn where the sound of water lulls guests to sleep each night.

What sets bed-and-breakfasts apart from other accommodations is the personalized attention and warm hospitality that make every stay feel special. Many hosts go out of their way to provide recommendations for local attractions, hiking trails, or lesser-known spots that might not appear in travel guides. Some offer customized experiences, such as wine tastings, home-cooked dinners, or private tours of historic properties. The sense of community and connection fostered in these settings adds to the charm, making each visit not just a stay, but a cherished memory.

No matter the style of accommodation chosen, lodging in the Ozarks offers something beyond just a place to sleep. Whether it's the refined elegance of a luxury resort, the rustic sophistication of a lodge, the solitude of a cabin, or the welcoming atmosphere of a bed-and-breakfast, every stay is enriched by the beauty of the region. The Ozarks' accommodations embrace the landscape, blending comfort with nature in a way that allows travelers to truly unwind and appreciate the slower, more intentional pace of life. With each sunrise over the hills, each crisp evening by the fire, and each morning filled with the sounds of birdsong, a stay in the Ozarks becomes not just a getaway, but an experience that lingers long after the journey ends.

Budget-Friendly Hotels & Motels

Unique Stays (Treehouses, Houseboats, etc.)

The Ozarks welcome travelers of all kinds, including those seeking comfortable and affordable accommodations that allow them to stretch their budget while still enjoying the beauty and adventure of the region. For budget-conscious visitors, the area offers an abundance of hotels and motels that provide clean, convenient, and well-located lodging without sacrificing essential amenities. Additionally, for those looking for a more unconventional overnight experience, the Ozarks offer a selection of unique stays that go beyond the traditional, with options such as treehouses suspended in the canopy, floating houseboats on serene lakes, and even repurposed train cars or yurts nestled in the wilderness.

For travelers seeking budget-friendly hotels and motels, the Ozarks provide an array of options that cater to different needs, whether it be a quick overnight stay, a centrally located base for day trips, or a family-friendly spot with extra conveniences. Chain hotels, which can be found in larger towns and cities such as Branson, Springfield, and Eureka Springs, offer familiar comfort with reliable service, often featuring free breakfasts, fitness centers, and swimming pools. These hotels are ideal for travelers who want a dependable stay with the added benefit of loyalty program perks or corporate discounts.

For those who prefer locally owned accommodations, independent motels and roadside inns provide an affordable alternative with a touch of Ozarks hospitality. Many of these establishments have been serving travelers for generations and boast a nostalgic charm reminiscent of classic road trips. Though simple, these motels often come with perks such as friendly owners who offer insider tips on hidden attractions, small courtyards where guests can relax in the evenings, or even direct access to nearby hiking trails or fishing spots. In smaller towns and rural areas, these independently run lodgings can often be found near scenic highways, providing easy access to the region's most picturesque landscapes.

Many budget-friendly hotels and motels in the Ozarks also cater to outdoor enthusiasts, offering designated spaces for boat parking, fishing gear storage, or even partnerships with local outfitters for discounted adventure packages. Travelers planning to spend their days hiking, exploring caves, or paddling along winding rivers will find these accommodations perfectly suited for their needs, as they allow for affordable lodging while ensuring convenience and accessibility to outdoor attractions.

Beyond traditional budget accommodations, the Ozarks are home to a variety of unique stays that provide an unforgettable overnight experience. One of the most sought-after options in recent years has been treehouse lodging, which allows guests to sleep among the treetops, immersed in nature without giving up modern comforts. These treehouses range from simple wooden structures with lofted sleeping areas and hammock decks to luxurious multi-level cabins with wraparound balconies, hot tubs, and panoramic windows that overlook lush forests or rivers. The seclusion and tranquility of treehouse stays make them particularly popular for couples seeking a romantic getaway, as well as families looking for a magical retreat where kids can wake up to birdsong and fall asleep beneath a sky full of stars.

Another one-of-a-kind accommodation option in the Ozarks is houseboat lodging, where visitors can experience the region's stunning lakes from the comfort of a floating home. Houseboats, available for rental on lakes such as Table Rock Lake and Lake of the Ozarks, come equipped with full kitchens, cozy sleeping quarters, and rooftop decks perfect for sunbathing or stargazing. Many houseboat rentals allow guests to cruise at their leisure, anchoring in quiet coves or docking at lakeside marinas for dinner and entertainment. This style of lodging is particularly popular among groups and families who want to combine relaxation with adventure, as it offers direct access to swimming, fishing, and water sports just steps from the door.

For travelers looking to embrace a more unconventional lifestyle, the Ozarks also offer stays in yurts, geodesic domes, and repurposed train cars. Yurts, inspired by traditional Mongolian nomadic dwellings, provide a unique blend of rustic simplicity and cozy charm. These circular tents, often found on the outskirts of state parks or tucked into quiet valleys, are furnished with comfortable bedding, wood-burning stoves, and skylights that allow for breathtaking nighttime views. Some yurt stays even include private decks with fire pits or hot tubs, making them a fantastic choice for travelers who want to stay connected to nature without sacrificing comfort.

For those with a love of history and vintage aesthetics, converted train car lodgings offer a nostalgic retreat. These railcars, often restored with period decor and antique furnishings, transport guests back in time while providing all the modern amenities needed for a comfortable stay. Found in select locations throughout the Ozarks, these stays appeal to train enthusiasts, history buffs, and those simply looking for a novel experience that stands apart from traditional lodging.

Boutique tiny homes and off-grid cabins also have a growing presence in the Ozarks, catering to travelers who appreciate minimalist living and eco-friendly accommodations. These compact but thoughtfully designed dwellings feature clever space-saving layouts, often incorporating elements such as lofted sleeping areas, floor-to-ceiling windows, and foldable furniture. Many of these rentals prioritize sustainability, utilizing solar power, composting toilets, and rainwater collection systems. Located in scenic areas with breathtaking views, these tiny homes provide a peaceful escape from the hustle and bustle of daily life while maintaining a small environmental footprint.

For those drawn to the romance of the open prairie or rolling farmland, farm stays offer an immersive rural experience that allows guests to participate in daily farm life while enjoying cozy accommodations. These stays, which range from charming guest cottages to rustic converted barns, give visitors the chance to interact with animals, pick fresh produce from the garden, and learn about sustainable farming practices. Many farm stays also offer home-cooked breakfasts featuring farm-fresh eggs, homemade jams, and locally sourced honey, creating a warm and welcoming atmosphere that feels like stepping into a simpler way of life.

Regardless of whether a traveler chooses a budget-friendly motel, a treetop retreat, a floating houseboat, or a historic train car, the Ozarks offer accommodations that cater to a wide range of preferences and budgets. The diversity of lodging options ensures that every visitor can find the perfect place to rest after a day of adventure, whether it be an affordable roadside inn with easy access to hiking trails or a one-of-a-kind stay that turns an overnight visit into a memorable experience. Each accommodation type contributes to the region's character, offering a place not just to sleep, but to fully embrace the natural beauty, history, and charm that define the Ozarks.

10. Hidden Gems & Off-the-Beaten-Path Spots

Underrated Hikes & Natural Wonders

Secret Swimming Holes & Caves

The Ozarks are known for their breathtaking landscapes, but beyond the well-traveled paths and famous viewpoints lie hidden treasures waiting to be discovered by those willing to venture off the beaten track. While many visitors flock to popular hiking trails and scenic destinations, the region's lesser-known trails and natural wonders offer just as much beauty, often with the added advantage of solitude and a deeper sense of connection to nature. From quiet forested paths leading to stunning waterfalls to secluded caves and pristine swimming holes tucked away in the wilderness, these hidden gems provide an opportunity for adventure seekers and nature lovers to experience the untouched side of the Ozarks.

Some of the most underrated hikes in the region take visitors through landscapes just as dramatic as the more well-known trails but with fewer crowds. One such trail winds through dense hardwood forests before emerging at a secluded bluff overlooking a valley of rolling hills. In the spring, the trail bursts into color with wildflowers lining the path, while autumn transforms the same landscape into a vibrant canvas of reds, oranges, and golds. Hikers who explore these lesser-traveled routes are often rewarded with incredible views, wildlife sightings, and the peaceful sounds of nature undisturbed by the foot traffic of popular destinations.

Another hidden hiking treasure is a narrow canyon trail where towering rock walls guide the way to a cascading waterfall that remains a well-kept secret among locals. Unlike the widely photographed falls that draw crowds during peak seasons, this one remains quiet year-round, with only the rustling of leaves and the gentle flow of water breaking the silence. The trail follows a small creek that meanders through the forest, requiring hikers to step across smooth stones and navigate wooden bridges along the way. The reward at the end of the trail is a stunning waterfall that tumbles down a moss-covered rock face into a crystal-clear pool, creating a perfect spot for reflection or a refreshing dip on a warm day.

In addition to hidden waterfalls, the Ozarks are home to secret swimming holes that offer some of the most pristine waters in the region. Unlike the well-known lakes and rivers that draw large crowds in the summer, these tucked-away spots provide a peaceful escape where visitors can cool off in natural pools surrounded by towering bluffs and dense foliage. Some of these swimming holes require a short hike to reach, adding to their secluded charm. On hot summer days, the water in these hidden pockets remains cool and inviting, shaded by towering sycamore trees that filter the sunlight into dappled patterns on the surface. Many of these spots are known only to those who have spent years exploring the region, their locations passed down through word-of-mouth rather than marked on maps or guidebooks.

Some of the most spectacular hidden swimming holes are found within deep gorges where streams carve out pockets of emerald water, forming perfect natural pools beneath overhanging rock formations. These areas, often formed by centuries of erosion, create breathtaking landscapes that feel like secret worlds. With their untouched beauty, they provide an incredible setting for an afternoon of relaxation or quiet contemplation. The water in these pools is often so clear that visitors can see the smooth river stones beneath the surface, and during the early morning hours, mist rising from the water adds a magical quality to the surroundings.

Beyond hidden trails and swimming holes, the Ozarks are also home to an extensive network of caves, many of which remain undiscovered by mainstream travelers. While a few well-known caves in the region attract visitors with guided tours and lighting displays, numerous smaller caves exist in remote areas, waiting to be explored by those with a sense of adventure. These limestone caverns, often nestled within steep hillsides or hidden behind waterfalls, contain intricate rock formations, underground streams, and chambers filled with fascinating geological features. Some require scrambling over rocky terrain or wading through shallow pools to enter, but for those who make the effort, they offer a glimpse into a world untouched by time.

One particularly fascinating cave remains hidden behind a small waterfall, its entrance concealed by a veil of flowing water. Reaching it requires following a narrow, winding path along a creek bed, where smooth stones and twisted tree roots make for an adventurous journey. Once inside, visitors find themselves in a cool, shadowy chamber where dripping stalactites and glowing minerals create an otherworldly atmosphere. Exploring these hidden caves allows visitors to step into a realm shaped by thousands of years of natural forces, where every curve of stone tells a story of the ancient past.

For those willing to go even further off the grid, the Ozarks hold otherworldly rock formations and geological wonders that few people ever see. In some remote areas, entire sections of forest open up to reveal towering rock pillars that have been sculpted by wind and water over millennia. These formations, with their unusual shapes and precariously balanced boulders, create landscapes that feel like something out of a fantasy novel. Hikers who explore these areas often feel as though they've stumbled upon a long-lost world, untouched by modern development.

Another remarkable hidden wonder is a stretch of riverbank where, after heavy rains, the water glows with a vibrant blue-green hue due to natural minerals present in the rock beneath the surface. The phenomenon is fleeting, appearing only under the right conditions, but those lucky enough to witness it describe it as an almost mystical experience. These rare natural occurrences make the Ozarks a constantly changing landscape, where even those who have spent a lifetime exploring the region can still discover something new.

Perhaps the most rewarding aspect of seeking out the Ozarks' lesser-known trails, swimming holes, and caves is the sense of discovery that comes with each new find. These hidden gems are places where nature remains wild and untouched, where visitors can experience the landscape as it has existed for centuries. They offer a deeper connection to the land, free from the distractions of crowded tourist spots or developed recreation areas. For those who take the time to explore beyond the usual destinations, the Ozarks reveal themselves in ways that are unexpected and unforgettable.

Exploring these hidden locations requires respect for nature and a sense of responsibility to preserve them for future generations. Many of these places are fragile ecosystems, home to rare plant species and delicate rock formations that have taken thousands of years to form. Visitors who tread lightly, leave no trace, and share knowledge of these places responsibly help ensure that these wonders remain unspoiled. The beauty of these secluded hikes, secret swimming spots, and mysterious caves lies in their pristine state, and it is up to those who discover them to help keep them that way.

The Ozarks are a region of endless discovery, where even the most experienced explorers can uncover new wonders with every visit. While the well-known destinations have their own undeniable charm, it is the hidden corners of this landscape that offer the most profound experiences. For those willing to take the path less traveled, the reward is a world of untouched beauty, waiting to be explored.

Quirky Roadside Attractions

Local Legends & Mysterious Places

The Ozarks are home to a fascinating array of roadside attractions, each with its own unique charm, eccentricity, and sense of nostalgia. From towering fiberglass figures and unusual museums to peculiar landmarks that seem plucked from another time, these quirky stops along the region's highways and backroads capture the spirit of a bygone era when road trips were an adventure in themselves. Many of these oddities have survived for decades, attracting curious travelers who delight in their offbeat appeal and the stories they hold. Some are well-known to those who frequent the region, while others remain hidden gems, stumbled upon by those willing to take detours off the main roads.

Among the most striking roadside attractions is a giant hillbilly statue that has stood as a beacon for passing motorists for generations. This towering figure, dressed in overalls and a wide-brimmed hat, once served as an advertisement for a long-gone tourist attraction but has since become a beloved fixture along the highway. It's a prime example of the kind of kitschy Americana that defined mid-century roadside culture, a relic from a time when oversized figures and exaggerated folk imagery were used to lure travelers into roadside diners, souvenir shops, and theme parks.

Not far from this towering roadside icon, an unusual rock formation known as the "Gravity Hill" has long puzzled visitors who stop to test its strange phenomenon. Here, cars left in neutral appear to roll uphill rather than down, defying logic and leaving those who witness it scratching their heads. The scientific explanation may lie in an optical illusion created by the surrounding landscape, but for many, the experience feels nothing short of magical. Over the years, legends have sprung up about ghostly forces at work, adding an extra layer of mystery to this already peculiar site.

In another part of the region, a roadside museum dedicated to the history of arcades and pinball machines transports visitors to the golden age of coin-operated entertainment. Housed in what was once a general store, this collection boasts dozens of vintage machines, many of which are still playable. It's a place where generations come together, as older visitors reminisce about their childhoods while younger guests marvel at the flashing lights and mechanical sounds of a pre-digital gaming era. The museum is a testament to the enduring appeal of simple, hands-on fun, and those who visit often find themselves lingering far longer than expected.

While the Ozarks are filled with charming oddities, they are also steeped in eerie legends and mysterious places that have sparked curiosity and intrigue for generations. One such location is a lonely stretch of road where travelers have reported ghostly apparitions and unexplained lights appearing in the night. Some say the glowing orbs that hover along the treetops are the spirits of long-lost settlers, while others insist they are nothing more than reflections from distant headlights. Regardless of the explanation, the stories persist, and the road has earned a reputation as one of the most haunted places in the region.

Deep within the forests of the Ozarks, another mystery unfolds in the form of an abandoned town, its few remaining structures slowly being reclaimed by nature. What little remains of this forgotten settlement consists of crumbling stone foundations, rusted machinery, and the occasional glimpse of a collapsed homestead. Those who visit often speak of an eerie silence that hangs over the place, as if the land itself remembers the people who once called it home. Some claim to have seen ghostly figures among the ruins, their outlines barely visible in the morning mist. While historians have pieced together fragments of the town's past, much about its sudden decline remains unknown, adding to the sense of mystery that surrounds it.

One of the region's most famous legends revolves around a supposed hidden treasure buried deep within the hills. According to the story, a notorious outlaw stashed a fortune in gold somewhere in the Ozarks before meeting an untimely end, leaving his riches undiscovered to this day. Over the years, treasure hunters armed with maps and metal detectors have scoured the area in search of the fabled hoard, but if the treasure exists, it has yet to be found. Some believe it is merely a tall tale, while others remain convinced that the gold lies buried beneath the dense forests, waiting for the right person to uncover it.

Further adding to the region's air of mystery are the tales of strange creatures said to roam the hills and hollows. Among the most famous of these is a shadowy figure known as the Ozark Howler, a beast described as having glowing red eyes, shaggy black fur, and a bone-chilling howl that echoes through the valleys at night. Skeptics dismiss the legend as mere folklore, but those who claim to have encountered the creature tell of a terrifying presence that defies explanation. Whether fact or fiction, the stories continue to be passed down, ensuring that the Ozark Howler remains a source of fascination and fear.

In addition to its supernatural tales, the region is also home to unexplained geological phenomena that have puzzled experts for years. One such site features a series of perfectly round depressions in the ground, known as "fairy circles," which have resisted scientific explanation. Theories range from ancient Native American ceremonial sites to natural sinkholes caused by underground water flow, but no definitive answer has ever been reached. Visitors who stumble upon these strange formations often remark on their almost unnatural symmetry and the unsettling quiet that surrounds them.

Another baffling location lies within a dense forest where, on certain nights, the trees seem to glow with an otherworldly light. Scientists attribute the phenomenon to bioluminescent fungi or naturally occurring phosphorescence, but those who have witnessed it firsthand describe it as something far more mystical. Legends tell of spirits guiding lost travelers with their ghostly illumination, while others believe it is a sign of hidden energies within the land itself. Regardless of the cause, those who experience it never forget the sight of trees shimmering under the darkness of the night.

The Ozarks have long been a place where the ordinary and the extraordinary blend together, where the past lingers just beneath the surface, and where legends continue to shape the region's identity. The quirky roadside attractions that dot the landscape serve as reminders of a time when road trips were as much about the journey as the destination, while the mysterious places hidden within the hills fuel a sense of wonder and curiosity. Whether drawn to the bizarre, the historic, or the unexplained, visitors to this region will find that the Ozarks hold stories unlike anywhere else—stories that continue to unfold with every turn in the road and every step into the unknown.

11. Practical Information

Safety Tips & Emergency

ContactsLocal Laws & Regulations

The Ozarks are a region of remarkable natural beauty, rich history, and welcoming communities, making it a wonderful place to explore. However, as with any travel destination, it is important to be well-prepared and informed about safety considerations, emergency procedures, and local regulations to ensure a smooth and enjoyable experience. While the area is generally safe for visitors, understanding the potential risks associated with outdoor activities, wildlife encounters, and regional laws will help travelers avoid unnecessary difficulties. Being mindful of these factors enhances not only personal safety but also the overall experience of exploring the Ozarks.

One of the most common safety concerns in the Ozarks is navigating the rugged terrain. Many visitors come to hike the region's extensive trail systems, which range from easy, well-maintained paths to more challenging backcountry routes. While the landscape is breathtaking, it can also be unforgiving. Steep inclines, rocky outcrops, and dense forested areas pose hazards, especially for those who are not accustomed to hiking in such conditions. Proper preparation, including wearing sturdy footwear, carrying sufficient water, and informing someone of planned routes, is essential. Sudden weather changes, particularly in the spring and fall, can make trails slippery and difficult to traverse. Checking the weather forecast before setting out and being prepared for changing conditions can prevent accidents and ensure a safe hiking experience.

Water activities, including boating, kayaking, and swimming, are major attractions in the Ozarks, with its many lakes, rivers, and springs drawing outdoor enthusiasts. While these activities provide endless enjoyment, they also require caution. Strong currents, hidden underwater obstacles, and rapidly changing water levels can pose risks, particularly in rivers such as the Buffalo National River. Life jackets should always be worn when engaging in water-based activities, and swimmers should be mindful of designated swimming areas to avoid unexpected hazards. Boat operators must be aware of local boating laws, including speed limits, no-wake zones, and alcohol restrictions, to prevent accidents and ensure the safety of everyone on the water.

Wildlife encounters are another aspect of outdoor adventure in the Ozarks that require awareness and respect. The region is home to a diverse range of wildlife, including black bears, snakes, and ticks, all of which can pose risks if not approached with caution. Black bear sightings are increasing in some areas, particularly in more remote regions, and while attacks are rare, it is crucial to store food properly when camping and avoid approaching or feeding wildlife. Snakes, including venomous species such as copperheads and rattlesnakes, are often found in rocky areas and near water sources. Wearing protective clothing and watching where one steps or places hands can reduce the risk of snakebites. Ticks, which are common in wooded and grassy areas, carry diseases such as Lyme disease and should be taken seriously. Using insect repellent, wearing long sleeves and pants, and checking for ticks after outdoor activities can help prevent bites and potential illness.

Driving in the Ozarks presents its own set of challenges, particularly for those unfamiliar with the winding mountain roads. While the scenery is stunning, it can be easy to become distracted. Sharp curves, sudden elevation changes, and narrow rural roads require careful attention and defensive driving. Wildlife, particularly deer, are commonly seen crossing roads, especially at dawn and dusk. Staying alert and driving at safe speeds can prevent accidents caused by unexpected animal crossings. Additionally, cell phone service can be unreliable in some remote areas, making it advisable to have a physical map or GPS device on hand.

In case of an emergency, knowing the appropriate contacts and response procedures is vital. Emergency services, including police, fire, and medical assistance, can be reached by dialing 911. However, in more remote areas where cell service may be spotty, having a backup plan, such as a whistle or signaling device, can be useful in attracting attention. Hospitals and urgent care centers are available in larger towns and cities, while rural areas may have limited medical facilities. Travelers with specific medical needs should plan accordingly and carry necessary medications at all times. Park rangers and visitor center staff can also provide assistance and information in case of an emergency, making it a good practice to check in with them before heading into more isolated areas.

Understanding local laws and regulations is just as important as knowing safety precautions. Many aspects of life in the Ozarks are governed by state and local laws that visitors should be aware of to avoid unintentional violations. Alcohol regulations, for example, vary by county, with some areas enforcing strict restrictions on sales and consumption. It is advisable to check local laws before purchasing or consuming alcohol, particularly in dry counties where alcohol sales are prohibited.

Camping regulations differ depending on whether a site is located in a state park, national forest, or private campground. Dispersed camping, which allows for setting up camp outside designated areas, is permitted in some areas but comes with restrictions to protect natural resources. Campers should follow Leave No Trace principles, which include packing out all trash, minimizing campfire impact, and respecting wildlife. Fire safety is especially critical during dry seasons when the risk of wildfires is high. Many areas require permits for campfires, and restrictions may be in place depending on weather conditions. Checking with park officials before lighting a fire ensures compliance with local regulations and helps prevent accidental wildfires.

Fishing and hunting are popular activities in the Ozarks, but they require proper licensing and adherence to specific regulations. State-issued fishing and hunting licenses are mandatory, and each state in the region has its own set of rules regarding season dates, bag limits, and permissible equipment. Conservation officers regularly patrol lakes and hunting grounds to ensure compliance, and violators can face fines or other penalties. Those unfamiliar with the regulations should consult state wildlife agencies for the most up-to-date information before engaging in these activities.

Respect for private property is another important consideration when exploring the Ozarks. Much of the land in the region is privately owned, and trespassing is taken seriously. While there are vast areas of public land available for recreation, visitors should always be mindful of property boundaries and seek permission before entering privately owned areas. Signs indicating private land should be respected, and in cases where permission is granted to explore, travelers should follow any guidelines set by the landowner.

Drones have become increasingly popular for capturing the breathtaking landscapes of the Ozarks, but their use is subject to regulations. Many state and national parks have restrictions on drone usage to protect wildlife and ensure a peaceful experience for visitors. Before flying a drone, it is important to check local policies and obtain necessary permits if required. Flying drones over private property without permission is prohibited, and care should be taken to avoid interfering with wildlife, particularly nesting birds and other sensitive species.

Being prepared and knowledgeable about local laws and safety considerations ensures a hassle-free and enjoyable experience in the Ozarks. The region's vast wilderness and unique communities offer endless opportunities for exploration, but they also require travelers to approach their adventures with responsibility and respect. By staying informed about emergency procedures, following safety guidelines for outdoor activities, and adhering to local regulations, visitors can fully immerse themselves in all that the Ozarks have to offer while ensuring a safe and memorable journey.

Accessibility & Travel Considerations

Packing Tips for Every Season

Traveling through the Ozarks is an enriching experience filled with breathtaking scenery, rich cultural heritage, and a variety of outdoor adventures. However, to ensure a smooth and enjoyable journey, it is important to consider accessibility and travel logistics. The region is known for its rugged landscapes, winding roads, and remote areas, all of which can present unique challenges for travelers with specific mobility needs or those requiring additional planning. From finding accommodations that cater to accessibility requirements to understanding the best ways to navigate the terrain, being prepared helps ensure that all visitors can fully experience the beauty of the Ozarks without unnecessary obstacles.

One of the key aspects of accessibility in the Ozarks is the availability of accommodations that cater to individuals with disabilities or mobility concerns. Larger cities such as Springfield, Branson, and Fayetteville offer a range of hotels with ADA-compliant rooms, wheelchair-accessible entrances, and other necessary amenities. Many modern lodgings provide elevators, roll-in showers, and widened doorways to accommodate those with mobility aids. However, in more rural areas and within state and national parks, accessible accommodations can be limited. Cabins, lodges, and campgrounds vary in terms of accessibility, with some offering paved pathways and adapted facilities while others are located in more rugged, uneven environments. It is always advisable to call ahead and confirm accessibility features before booking, as even listings that claim to be accessible may have limitations, such as gravel parking areas or steps at entrances.

For those interested in exploring the region's natural wonders, numerous parks and recreational areas have made efforts to improve accessibility. Many of the most popular attractions, such as state parks and scenic overlooks, offer paved or boardwalk-style trails that allow for easier navigation. Some of the best accessible nature experiences include the Springfield Conservation Nature Center, which has a paved, wheelchair-friendly trail through beautiful woodlands, and the accessible pathways at Dogwood Canyon Nature Park, which allow visitors to enjoy waterfalls and wildlife without the challenge of steep or uneven terrain. Some national parks and wildlife refuges also offer all-terrain wheelchairs or tram tours for those who need assistance exploring the more rugged areas. While not all hiking trails in the Ozarks are suitable for those with mobility impairments, several trails have been designed or modified to accommodate visitors with varying abilities.

Transportation considerations are also an important factor in planning a trip through the Ozarks. While major highways provide easy access to cities and towns, the region's more rural and mountainous areas can present challenges for those unaccustomed to driving on steep, curving roads. Rental cars are the most flexible option for visitors who want to explore beyond city centers, but it is important to note that some rental agencies may not offer vehicles with adaptive driving modifications. For those who rely on public transportation, options are limited outside of larger cities. Springfield and Fayetteville have public bus systems, and Branson offers trolley services to key attractions, but rural areas generally lack public transit. Ride-sharing services such as Uber and Lyft operate in some towns, but availability can be inconsistent. Travelers needing accessible transportation should check ahead to confirm whether taxis or specialized transport services are available in their destinations.

Packing appropriately for a trip to the Ozarks is another crucial aspect of travel preparation. The region experiences all four seasons, with each bringing its own unique climate considerations. Packing the right clothing and gear ensures comfort and safety, whether visiting during the warm summer months or the crisp autumn season.

Spring in the Ozarks can be unpredictable, with warm days and cool nights, as well as occasional rain showers. Packing lightweight, breathable clothing is ideal for daytime activities, while a light jacket or fleece is recommended for the cooler evenings. Waterproof gear, including a rain jacket and sturdy shoes, is essential, as sudden storms are common, particularly in March and April. Those planning on hiking or engaging in outdoor activities should also bring insect repellent, as mosquitoes and ticks become active during the warmer months.

Summer brings hot temperatures, often reaching the upper 80s and 90s, with high humidity. Light, moisture-wicking clothing is essential to stay cool and comfortable. Sunglasses, a hat, and sunscreen are necessary to protect against the intense sun, especially for those spending time on the water or hiking in open areas. Hydration is crucial, so carrying a reusable water bottle is recommended. Many of the region's lakes and rivers become popular destinations in the summer, making swimsuits, water shoes, and quick-drying towels useful additions to any packing list.

Fall is one of the most popular times to visit the Ozarks, thanks to the breathtaking foliage and mild temperatures. Days are often warm, but mornings and evenings can be chilly, making layered clothing the best option. A warm sweater or jacket is necessary, especially in October and November when temperatures begin to drop significantly. Comfortable hiking boots are ideal for exploring trails covered in fallen leaves, which can sometimes be slippery. Since fall is also a prime time for camping, those planning overnight stays in the wilderness should bring a warm sleeping bag, as nighttime temperatures can dip below freezing in higher elevations.

Winter in the Ozarks is relatively mild compared to northern states, but it can still bring cold temperatures, especially in December and January. Snowfall is less common in lower elevations but does occur in the higher mountains, occasionally making roads icy or difficult to navigate. Warm, insulated clothing, gloves, and a hat are essential for outdoor activities. Those visiting during winter should also check weather forecasts frequently, as sudden cold snaps or winter storms can impact travel plans. Heated lodging options are widely available, but for those camping or spending extended time outdoors, proper cold-weather gear is necessary.

Packing considerations also extend beyond clothing, as the type of gear and supplies needed can vary depending on the activities planned. For those exploring the Ozarks' extensive trail systems, a good pair of hiking boots, a backpack with essential supplies, and a map or GPS device are crucial. Many rural areas have limited cell service, so having a physical map or downloading offline navigation apps can prevent getting lost. For those engaging in water-based activities, dry bags to protect electronics, a waterproof phone case, and a personal flotation device are highly recommended.

Regardless of the season, having a basic first aid kit is a good idea, especially for those venturing into remote areas. Minor injuries such as blisters, insect bites, and scrapes are common, so carrying bandages, antiseptic wipes, and pain relievers can be helpful. Travelers with specific medical needs should ensure they have an adequate supply of prescription medications, as pharmacies may be limited in some rural areas.

Being well-prepared and considering accessibility needs, transportation options, and seasonal packing requirements will help ensure a seamless and enjoyable experience in the Ozarks. Thoughtful planning allows travelers to fully embrace the region's natural beauty and cultural offerings while minimizing potential challenges. Whether taking in scenic mountain views, exploring charming historic towns, or immersing in outdoor adventures, having the right knowledge and essentials makes for a truly memorable journey.

12. Suggested Itineraries

Weekend Getaway

A weekend getaway to the Ozarks offers a perfect blend of relaxation, adventure, and cultural immersion, making it an ideal escape for travelers seeking a break from their daily routine. With its rolling hills, serene lakes, historic towns, and abundant outdoor activities, the region provides an ideal setting for a short but fulfilling trip. Whether visitors are looking for a peaceful retreat in nature, an exciting itinerary packed with entertainment, or a romantic weekend with scenic backdrops, the Ozarks cater to a wide range of interests and travel styles. Careful planning ensures that even a short stay is packed with memorable experiences, allowing visitors to make the most of their time in this diverse and scenic region.

One of the key decisions when planning a weekend trip to the Ozarks is selecting the right destination. For those seeking a vibrant and entertainment-filled experience, Branson is an excellent choice, offering live music, world-class attractions, and bustling shopping districts. Visitors looking for a more tranquil retreat may find Eureka Springs to be the perfect spot, with its historic charm, Victorian architecture, and winding streets lined with unique boutiques and art galleries. Nature lovers may opt for the Lake of the Ozarks or the Buffalo National River, where they can immerse themselves in breathtaking landscapes, water activities, and scenic hikes. Each area of the Ozarks has its own character, making it important to align travel preferences with the chosen destination to ensure a well-balanced and enjoyable weekend.

For those looking to make the most of a short trip, arriving on a Friday evening allows for an early start on Saturday, maximizing the time available to explore. Checking into a cozy cabin, a lakeside resort, or a boutique inn immediately sets the tone for the weekend. Many accommodations in the Ozarks offer scenic settings that enhance the experience, whether it be a secluded log cabin tucked into the hills or a lodge with stunning sunset views over the water. Settling in on the first night provides an opportunity to unwind, enjoy a leisurely dinner at a local restaurant, and map out the activities for the next two days.

Saturday is often the busiest day of a weekend getaway, offering a full day to explore the highlights of the chosen destination. In Branson, a morning might begin with a scenic breakfast at a café overlooking Table Rock Lake, followed by a visit to Silver Dollar City for thrilling rides and old-fashioned Ozarks culture. Alternatively, those in Eureka Springs may start with a peaceful morning stroll through the historic district, admiring the preserved 19th-century buildings and stopping at local shops. For those visiting the Lake of the Ozarks, an early morning boat rental or guided fishing tour is a great way to experience the vast beauty of the water.

Outdoor enthusiasts often prefer to spend the day hiking, kayaking, or exploring the many natural wonders of the region. The Buffalo National River offers some of the best paddling experiences in the country, with towering bluffs and pristine waters that provide an unmatched sense of serenity. The Ozark National Forest has an abundance of trails leading to breathtaking overlooks and hidden waterfalls, making it a prime destination for hikers looking to experience the untouched beauty of the area. Those interested in underground exploration can visit one of the many caves in the region, such as Marvel Cave near Branson or Cosmic Cavern in northern Arkansas, where fascinating rock formations and underground lakes provide a unique adventure.

After a full day of activities, a relaxing evening is the perfect way to unwind and reflect on the day's experiences. A lakeside dinner, a cozy campfire, or a visit to a local winery or brewery provides the ideal setting for winding down. Branson's famous live shows offer high-energy performances that entertain audiences of all ages, while Eureka Springs' intimate music venues and art-centric atmosphere provide a more low-key cultural experience. Those looking for a peaceful retreat may choose to stargaze from a cabin porch or take a quiet walk along the shores of one of the many lakes and rivers.

Sunday morning allows for a more relaxed itinerary, with a late breakfast or brunch at a beloved local eatery. Many towns in the Ozarks offer charming diners and cafés serving traditional Southern fare, homemade biscuits, and locally roasted coffee. Those who want to make the most of their final hours might opt for a scenic drive, such as the Pig Trail Scenic Byway or the Ozark Mountain Highroad, both of which offer breathtaking views and picturesque pull-off points. Others may choose to visit a historic site, such as Wilson's Creek National Battlefield or the Thorncrown Chapel, for a meaningful and contemplative end to the trip.

For visitors looking to bring a piece of the Ozarks home with them, a stop at a local artisan shop, farmers' market, or antique store can be a wonderful way to commemorate the weekend. Handmade pottery, locally crafted candles, and unique antiques are just a few of the treasures that travelers can find as lasting reminders of their time in the region. Many shops feature work from Ozarks artists, ranging from handwoven textiles to intricate woodwork, allowing visitors to support local craftspeople while finding one-of-a-kind souvenirs.

A weekend getaway in the Ozarks offers an escape into a world of natural beauty, rich culture, and warm hospitality. Whether choosing an action-packed itinerary filled with adventure or a peaceful retreat focused on relaxation, the region provides countless opportunities to create lasting memories. With just a few days in the Ozarks, visitors can experience the essence of this remarkable area, leaving with a deeper appreciation for its landscapes, history, and vibrant local communities. Proper planning ensures that every moment is well spent, making a short trip feel both rewarding and immersive. The magic of the Ozarks is that even in a brief visit, the experience lingers long after departure, inspiring travelers to return time and time again.

One-Week Road Trip

Family-Friendly Adventures

A one-week road trip through the Ozarks provides an unforgettable journey through some of the most breathtaking landscapes and culturally rich destinations in the region. With its winding mountain roads, serene lakes, charming historic towns, and diverse outdoor activities, the Ozarks are an ideal setting for an immersive road trip experience. Travelers can enjoy a mix of scenic drives, nature exploration, entertainment, and local culture, ensuring a well-rounded itinerary filled with adventure and relaxation. Careful planning allows for a balanced pace, ensuring that each destination is thoroughly enjoyed without feeling rushed.

The journey often begins in Springfield, Missouri, a gateway city to the Ozarks that offers an ideal starting point. With its blend of urban convenience and small-town charm, Springfield provides a perfect introduction to the region. A visit to the Fantastic Caverns, America's only ride-through cave, sets the tone for the natural wonders ahead. History lovers can explore the Wilson's Creek National Battlefield, while families may enjoy the Wonders of Wildlife National Museum & Aquarium, a world-class attraction showcasing marine life and conservation efforts. After a day of exploration, a short drive south leads to Branson, a destination known for its live entertainment and lakeside beauty.

Branson offers an exciting mix of attractions that cater to all interests. A morning visit to Silver Dollar City immerses travelers in the Ozarks' heritage with thrilling rides, live music, artisan demonstrations, and delicious traditional foods. The city's vibrant entertainment district offers a variety of shows, from country music and comedy acts to magic performances and acrobatics. The scenic beauty of Table Rock Lake provides a peaceful contrast to the bustling city, with opportunities for boating, fishing, or simply enjoying a lakeside sunset. Exploring the Branson Landing shopping and dining district offers a lively end to the day before continuing the journey deeper into the Ozarks.

A road trip through the Ozarks would not be complete without experiencing the natural beauty of the Buffalo National River in northern Arkansas. This preserved riverway is a paradise for outdoor enthusiasts, offering breathtaking hiking trails, pristine waters for canoeing and kayaking, and towering bluffs that define the landscape. A float trip down the Buffalo River provides a chance to encounter local wildlife, from soaring bald eagles to grazing elk. The historic town of Jasper, nestled along the river, serves as an excellent base for exploring nearby waterfalls, including Hemmed-In Hollow, the tallest waterfall between the Rockies and the Appalachians.

Continuing eastward, Eureka Springs is a must-visit stop on a road trip through the Ozarks. This uniquely preserved Victorian town is known for its winding, hilly streets, art galleries, historic buildings, and therapeutic natural springs. A stroll through the downtown area reveals an eclectic mix of boutiques, cafes, and antique shops, offering an opportunity to experience the town's creative and cultural charm. The Thorncrown Chapel, an architectural marvel nestled in the woods, provides a serene retreat for visitors seeking tranquility. Ghost tours and underground cave explorations add an element of mystery to the town's already enchanting atmosphere.

For travelers seeking a different side of the Ozarks, the journey can continue to the Lake of the Ozarks, a vast reservoir that serves as one of the Midwest's most popular recreational destinations. Whether staying in a lakefront resort, a cozy cabin, or an RV park, the area provides endless opportunities for water activities, from jet skiing and paddleboarding to fishing and leisurely cruises. Ha Ha Tonka State Park, with its castle ruins and dramatic karst landscapes, offers stunning hiking trails and panoramic views of the lake. A drive along the winding roads surrounding the lake reveals hidden coves, scenic overlooks, and charming waterfront restaurants.

A final stop on this week-long journey may include a return north through smaller towns and scenic byways, stopping at lesser-known gems such as the Ozark National Scenic Riverways in southern Missouri. This area offers clear, spring-fed rivers perfect for floating, as well as historic sites like Alley Spring Mill, where visitors can witness the beauty of a natural spring feeding into a vibrant turquoise pool. Driving through the region's rolling hills and lush forests provides a fitting end to the journey, allowing travelers to soak in the beauty of the Ozarks one last time before heading home.

For families embarking on an Ozarks adventure, the region provides an abundance of family-friendly activities that cater to all ages. From thrilling theme parks and interactive museums to hands-on outdoor experiences, the Ozarks ensure that young travelers remain engaged and entertained throughout the trip. A carefully planned itinerary allows families to strike a balance between adventure, relaxation, and educational experiences, making the trip both fun and enriching.

Branson is a top destination for family-friendly fun, offering attractions such as Silver Dollar City, which combines amusement park thrills with immersive Ozarks heritage experiences. The park's live demonstrations of blacksmithing, glassblowing, and traditional crafts provide a fascinating look into the region's history while still offering excitement through roller coasters and water rides. The Butterfly Palace & Rainforest Adventure allows children to step into a tropical environment filled with thousands of butterflies, interactive exhibits, and reptile encounters. A visit to the Titanic Museum in Branson adds an educational component to the trip, with hands-on exhibits that bring history to life.

Table Rock Lake provides countless opportunities for family bonding, whether through a relaxing day at Moonshine Beach, a guided fishing excursion, or an afternoon spent tubing and wakeboarding on the water. The Showboat Branson Belle, a riverboat-style cruise, combines dining, entertainment, and scenic views in a way that delights both children and adults. Families looking for a more relaxed pace can explore the Shepherd of the Hills Fish Hatchery, where kids can feed the trout and learn about conservation efforts in the area.

The Ozarks also provide a playground for young adventurers who love the great outdoors. Families can explore kid-friendly hiking trails such as the Lost Canyon Cave and Nature Trail, which offers breathtaking views and waterfalls along an easy-to-navigate path. Caving adventures at Fantastic Caverns allow visitors to ride through an underground wonderland, making it accessible to young children and those with mobility concerns. For a more hands-on nature experience, the Dogwood Canyon Nature Park offers tram tours where families can see bison, elk, and longhorn cattle in a beautiful preserve.

Wildlife encounters are a highlight of family-friendly adventures in the Ozarks. The Promised Land Zoo in Branson features interactive exhibits, where children can feed kangaroos, pet baby goats, and even get up close to exotic animals like sloths and lemurs. The National Tiger Sanctuary offers guided tours where families can learn about big cats and the sanctuary's conservation efforts. For those who prefer to see wildlife in their natural habitat, the elk herd at Boxley Valley in the Buffalo National River area provides an unforgettable experience, especially in the early morning and late evening hours.

As the trip comes to an end, families often reflect on the unique experiences that have made their time in the Ozarks special. Whether it's the excitement of a theme park ride, the peacefulness of a lakeside sunset, the wonder of exploring a cave, or the simple joy of roasting marshmallows around a campfire, the Ozarks create cherished memories that last a lifetime. The region's blend of outdoor adventure, cultural attractions, and small-town charm ensures that every family member finds something to love, making it an ideal destination for a fun-filled and rewarding vacation.

Romantic Retreats

Outdoor Enthusiast's Dream

The Ozarks provide the perfect setting for romantic retreats, with their breathtaking landscapes, charming small towns, and secluded getaways offering couples an escape from the busyness of everyday life. Whether it's a cozy cabin nestled in the mountains, a luxury resort with spa services, or a lakeside retreat with stunning sunset views, the region offers countless opportunities for couples to reconnect and create unforgettable memories. The natural beauty of the Ozarks, combined with intimate dining options, adventure-filled activities, and relaxing experiences, makes it an ideal destination for those seeking romance in a tranquil and scenic environment.

A romantic getaway in the Ozarks often begins with choosing the perfect setting. Secluded cabins and boutique bed-and-breakfasts provide a cozy and intimate atmosphere, allowing couples to unwind in the midst of nature. Many of these accommodations come with private hot tubs, fireplaces, and panoramic views of the surrounding mountains or lakes. Staying in a remote cabin near the Buffalo National River allows for complete immersion in the beauty of the outdoors, while resorts near Table Rock Lake provide luxurious amenities with easy access to water activities. Eureka Springs, with its Victorian charm and historic inns, offers an enchanting experience for couples who appreciate quaint streets, art galleries, and candlelit dining.

Outdoor experiences add an element of adventure to a romantic retreat. A sunrise or sunset hike along scenic trails, such as Whitaker Point in Arkansas or the Top of the Rock Lost Canyon Trail in Missouri, offers breathtaking views and quiet moments to share together. For those who enjoy the serenity of the water, a private boat ride on one of the region's pristine lakes can be a magical experience. Table Rock Lake and the Lake of the Ozarks provide opportunities for sunset cruises, where couples can toast to their love while drifting across the calm waters. Kayaking along the Buffalo River offers a peaceful and intimate way to explore the region's natural wonders, with towering bluffs and hidden waterfalls creating a picturesque setting.

Dining is an essential part of any romantic escape, and the Ozarks provide a variety of options that cater to different tastes. Farm-to-table restaurants, charming cafes, and upscale dining establishments offer locally sourced ingredients and carefully crafted menus. In Eureka Springs, an evening spent at a historic fine dining restaurant with a candlelit setting creates an unforgettable experience. Branson's lakeside restaurants offer stunning waterfront views, where couples can enjoy fresh seafood or steak while watching the sun dip below the horizon. Wineries and breweries throughout the region provide intimate tastings and tours, allowing couples to savor locally produced wines or craft beers while enjoying the peaceful surroundings.

Relaxation is at the heart of many romantic retreats, and the Ozarks offer numerous ways to unwind and indulge. Many resorts and lodges feature full-service spas, where couples can enjoy side-by-side massages, facials, and other pampering treatments. Hot springs and mineral baths, found in locations such as Eureka Springs, provide a soothing and therapeutic experience. Some accommodations offer in-room spa services, allowing couples to enjoy a massage without ever having to leave the comfort of their private retreat.

The magic of a romantic getaway in the Ozarks is in the little details—the quiet walks through scenic parks, the spontaneous detours to hidden waterfalls, the shared laughter during a new adventure, and the moments of stillness under a starlit sky. Whether it's a weekend escape or a longer stay, the Ozarks provide the perfect backdrop for romance, making it an ideal destination for proposals, honeymoons, anniversaries, or simply a well-deserved retreat for two.

For those with a passion for the outdoors, the Ozarks serve as a dream destination filled with rugged landscapes, challenging trails, rushing rivers, and countless opportunities for adventure. From hiking and rock climbing to kayaking and caving, the region offers thrilling experiences for those who seek to immerse themselves in nature. The vast wilderness areas, protected national parks, and diverse terrain ensure that every outdoor enthusiast can find an activity that suits their interests and skill level.

Hiking in the Ozarks is an unforgettable experience, with trails that lead to breathtaking vistas, hidden waterfalls, and diverse ecosystems. The Buffalo National River area is home to some of the most stunning trails in the region, including the Hemmed-In Hollow Trail, which takes hikers to the tallest waterfall between the Rockies and the Appalachians. Whitaker Point, also known as Hawksbill Crag, is one of the most photographed spots in Arkansas and offers a spectacular panoramic view of the surrounding mountains. The Ozark Highlands Trail provides a more challenging adventure, spanning over 200 miles through forests, ridges, and valleys.

Rock climbing and bouldering enthusiasts will find plenty of opportunities to test their skills on the limestone bluffs and sandstone cliffs scattered throughout the Ozarks. Horseshoe Canyon Ranch is a premier climbing destination, with hundreds of routes for climbers of all experience levels. The Sam's Throne area also offers a variety of climbing challenges, with stunning views and rugged rock formations that make every ascent a rewarding experience.

For those who love water-based adventures, the rivers and lakes of the Ozarks provide endless possibilities. The Buffalo National River is a paddler's paradise, with miles of crystal-clear waters that wind through towering bluffs and dense forests. Canoeing or kayaking along the river allows outdoor enthusiasts to experience the beauty of the Ozarks from a unique perspective, with opportunities to spot wildlife such as deer, bald eagles, and river otters. The Current and Jacks Fork Rivers, part of the Ozark National Scenic Riverways, also offer incredible floating experiences, with spring-fed waters and scenic landscapes that make for a peaceful yet exhilarating journey.

Lakes such as Table Rock, Bull Shoals, and the Lake of the Ozarks provide ample opportunities for boating, fishing, and water sports. Anglers can try their luck catching bass, trout, and catfish in the clear waters, while wakeboarders and jet skiers can enjoy the thrill of speeding across the expansive lakes. Scuba diving in the Ozarks is also a unique experience, with several locations offering underwater exploration of sunken boats, caves, and hidden treasures beneath the surface.

Exploring caves and underground wonders is another highlight for outdoor enthusiasts in the Ozarks. The region is home to thousands of caves, some of which are open for guided tours and spelunking adventures. Blanchard Springs Caverns in Arkansas features stunning rock formations, underground rivers, and massive caverns that feel like a hidden world beneath the surface. Fantastic Caverns in Missouri offers a ride-through experience, allowing visitors to see incredible cave formations without extensive hiking. More adventurous cavers can explore less developed caves, where guided spelunking tours lead through narrow passageways and deep underground chambers.

Camping in the Ozarks allows adventurers to fully immerse themselves in the region's natural beauty. Whether it's pitching a tent along the Buffalo River, setting up camp in the Mark Twain National Forest, or staying in a rustic backcountry campsite, the options for spending a night under the stars are plentiful. For those who prefer a bit more comfort, many parks and campgrounds offer cabins, RV sites, and glamping experiences that combine outdoor adventure with modern amenities.

Wildlife enthusiasts will find the Ozarks to be a haven for observing diverse species in their natural habitats. The region is home to black bears, white-tailed deer, wild turkeys, and countless species of birds. Elk can often be spotted in the Boxley Valley area, particularly during the fall mating season when their calls echo through the valley. Guided wildlife tours and nature preserves offer opportunities to see these animals up close while learning about conservation efforts to protect the Ozarks' rich biodiversity.

The Ozarks are a paradise for those who love the outdoors, offering a playground of adventure, discovery, and unparalleled natural beauty. Whether scaling cliffs, paddling through winding rivers, hiking to scenic overlooks, or simply soaking in the serenity of the wilderness, the region provides unforgettable experiences that leave visitors longing to return.

13. Resources & Further Reading

Useful Websites & Travel Apps

Planning a trip to the Ozarks is an exciting endeavor, and utilizing the right digital tools can enhance the experience by providing valuable information, navigation assistance, and insights into local attractions. Several websites and mobile applications are particularly useful for travelers seeking to explore this picturesque region.

For comprehensive information on the Lake of the Ozarks area, the official tourism website serves as an excellent resource. It offers detailed guides on accommodations, dining options, outdoor activities, and upcoming events, helping visitors plan their stay effectively. The site also provides downloadable visitor guides and maps, ensuring travelers have access to essential information both online and offline.

To complement the website, the Lake of the Ozarks app is available for mobile devices. This application assists in planning vacations, weekend getaways, or day trips by offering features such as event calendars, attraction listings, and personalized itineraries. Its user-friendly interface makes it easy to discover new activities and manage travel plans on the go.

For those interested in exploring the Ozark Trail, the Ozark Trail Association's Trip Planner is an invaluable tool. It provides detailed itineraries, directions, and maps for various routes, catering to hikers, bikers, and equestrians. Users can customize their adventure by selecting the type of activity, trip length, pace, and route type, ensuring a tailored experience that matches their preferences and skill levels.

When navigating the expansive Ozark region, having reliable navigation tools is crucial. While many smartphones come equipped with built-in compass applications, additional apps can enhance outdoor navigation. For instance, Compass 360 Pro offers accurate location data and customization options, making it ideal for adventurers. However, it's important to note that some compass apps are exclusive to Android devices and may contain advertisements .

For road trip enthusiasts, the Roadtrippers app is a valuable resource. It assists travelers in planning their drives with real-time GPS updates, integration with popular mapping services, and reviews of local attractions. The app offers both free and premium versions, with the latter providing additional features such as the ability to add more stops to a single trip.

Additionally, the National Park Service mobile app is a one-stop shop for planning adventures in areas like the Buffalo National River. Created by park rangers, the app includes interactive maps, self-guided tours, information on park amenities, accessibility details, and offline use capabilities, making it a comprehensive guide for exploring national parks within the Ozarks .

By leveraging these websites and applications, travelers can enhance their journey through the Ozarks, ensuring they have access to up-to-date information, reliable navigation, and personalized recommendations that cater to their interests and needs.

Recommended Books & Documentaries

Social Media & Local Travel Groups

Exploring the rich cultural tapestry and natural beauty of the Ozarks can be greatly enhanced by delving into its literature, documentaries, and engaging with local communities through social media and travel groups. These resources offer diverse perspectives, historical insights, and practical information that can deepen one's appreciation and understanding of this unique region.

A foundational work that provides a comprehensive historical perspective is "A History of the Ozarks, Volume 1: The Old Ozarks" by Brooks Blevins. This volume is the first in a three-part series that delves into the geological formation, early inhabitants, and the socio-political developments that have shaped the Ozarks. Blevins meticulously traces the region's evolution from prehistoric times through the 19th century, offering readers a nuanced understanding of the forces that have influenced its development. His narrative weaves together the stories of Native American tribes, European settlers, and the economic and cultural transformations that have defined the area. This scholarly yet accessible work is essential for anyone seeking to comprehend the complex history of the Ozarks.

For those interested in the cultural and social aspects, "A Living History of the Ozarks" by Phyllis Rossiter serves as an engaging guide. Rossiter, a native of the region, explores the Ozarks through its landmarks and historical sites, providing readers with a tangible connection to its past. The book covers a wide array of topics, including the traditions, folklore, and daily life of the Ozark people. Rossiter's narrative is enriched with anecdotes and illustrations that bring the history of the region to life, making it a valuable resource for both visitors and residents alike.

In the realm of documentaries, "Water & Fire: A Story of the Ozarks" offers a visual and narrative exploration of the region's history and culture. Produced by PBS, this documentary delves into the lives of the people who have called the Ozarks home, highlighting their resilience and the unique challenges they have faced. Through interviews, historical footage, and stunning cinematography, "Water & Fire" paints a vivid picture of the Ozarks' past and present, providing viewers with a deeper appreciation of its rich heritage.

Engaging with local communities through social media platforms can also provide valuable insights and up-to-date information. The Facebook group "Travel The Ozarks" is a vibrant community where members share photographs, travel stories, historical anecdotes, and recommendations related to the Ozarks region. This group serves as a platform for both locals and visitors to exchange experiences, ask questions, and discover hidden gems within the area. Similarly, the "Love My OZARKS" Facebook group is dedicated to documenting all aspects of the Ozarks, including family stories, historical events, and notable places to visit. Participation in these groups can offer a more personal perspective and insider knowledge that may not be readily available through traditional travel guides.

For those seeking organized travel experiences, the Ozark Gateway's group travel services provide tailored itineraries and resources for exploring the region. They offer assistance in planning group tours, business retreats, and adventure outings, ensuring that travelers can experience the Ozarks' attractions in a structured and informative manner. Their services cater to a variety of interests, from historical tours to outdoor adventures, making them a valuable resource for planning a comprehensive visit to the area.

By immersing oneself in the literature, visual media, and community discussions centered on the Ozarks, travelers can gain a multifaceted understanding of the region. These resources not only inform but also enrich the travel experience, allowing for a deeper connection to the land and its people. Whether through the pages of a meticulously researched history book, the lens of a documentary filmmaker, or the shared experiences of fellow travelers, the Ozarks reveal themselves as a region of profound beauty, complexity, and enduring allure.

Made in the USA
Columbia, SC
14 May 2025

57922182R00093